PIAGET, PHILOSOPHY AND THE HUMAN SCIENCES

PIAGET
PHILOSOPHY
AND THE
HUMAN SCIENCES

Edited by
HUGH J. SILVERMAN

NORTHWESTERN UNIVERSITY PRESS
EVANSTON, IL

Northwestern University Press
Evanston, Illinois 60208-4210

First published in the United States of America in 1980 by Humanities Press
Inc., Atlantic Highlands, N.J., and in England by The Harvester Press Ltd.,
Brighton, Sussex. Copyright © 1980 by Humanities Press Inc. Northwestern
University Press edition published 1997 by arrangement with Hugh J.
Silverman. All rights reserved.

Printed in the United States of America

ISBN 0-8101-1497-6

Library of Congress Cataloging-in-Publication Data

Piaget, philosophy, and the human sciences / edited by Hugh J. Silverman.
      p. cm.
   Originally published: Atlantic Highlands, N.J. : Humanities Press ;
Brighton, Sussex : Harvester Press, 1980.
   Includes bibliographical references and index.
   ISBN 0-8101-1497-6 (paper : alk. paper)
   1. Piaget, Jean, 1896– . 2. Cognition. 3. Knowledge, Theory of. I. Silverman,
Hugh J.
BF311.P523P5 1997
153.4—dc21   97-2643
                                                                        CIP

The paper used in this publication meets the minimum requirements of the
American National Standard for Information Sciences—Permanence of Paper
for Printed Library Materials, ANSI Z39.48-1984.

Contents

ACKNOWLEDGEMENTS

At an early stage in the planning of the Stony Brook Conference on 'Piaget, Philosophy, and the Human Sciences,' I invited Professor Donn Welton to assist me in the organization and realization of the program. Although he took primary responsibility for the Faculty Seminar, I am grateful for his advice and help throughout the period leading to and resulting in a particularly exciting conference. James Winder and Steven Lappen worked hard on the transcriptions of discussion sessions. Without their efficient typing and good judgement, I would have been unable to edit the oral features of the program into a lasting document. The copy-editing skills of Pegi Thomas have been crucial in transforming the manuscript into a polished book. A number of other philosophy graduate students attended to the tape-recorders and to preparational details for the event itself. My wife, L. Theresa Silverman, herself a developmental psychologist, was always available for consultation and companionship at all stages of the project.

Application had been made to the Matchette Foundation for support of the program. Since funds were not forthcoming until a later date (and I am indebted to Robert B. Eckles, Secretary of the Foundation, for permitting the grant to be applied to another series of lectures at Stony Brook), Dean Herbert Weisinger provided the needed assistance to the Philosophy Department for the conference.

Finally, I wish to thank Don Ihde, Chairman of the Philosophy Department, for his welcome at the opening of the series of events in May 1977 and for his continued encouragement of this sort of enterprise. Most of the other faculty and students who had a role in 'Piaget, Philosophy, and the Human Sciences' are identified in one way or another in the discussion segments that follow each paper as well as in the course of the Faculty Seminar.

FOREWORD

Hugh J. Silverman

The papers and discussions included here originally took place at the State University of New York at Stony Brook on May 5-6, 1977. The two-day event followed in the order we have offered in this volume. Each of the papers was revised after the conference. All of the discussions following the presentations were transcribed and edited to conform to good sense. The Faculty Seminar is also an edited version of what transpired during an intensive two hours on Friday morning prior to the last three papers. As a whole, this book represents the significance of the fourth annual Stony Brook Studies in Philosophy conference, sponsored by the Department of Philosophy at Stony Brook.

This collection of essays and discussions goes far beyond a particular event which took place at a specific time. It stands on its own as a sustained inquiry into the relationship between the genetic epistemology of Jean Piaget, the various domains of philosophy, and the human sciences in general. The scope of the inquiry is interdisciplinary. It is organized in the form of a wheel — not the wheel of Fortune as medievals such as Boethius and Dante conceived of it — but the wheel of human knowledge.

The center or hub of this wheel is the elaboration of Piaget's fundamental positions on epistemology. Hans Furth, a noted authority on Piaget's work and a former research psychologist at the Institute in Geneva, sets forth the basic theses of Piaget's theory. Out of a long list of binary oppositions, including assimilation and accommodation, pre-operatory and operatory, pre-linguistic and linguistic, structure and genesis, knower and known, Furth sorts out the four basic stages of human development. He shows that within the context of a basic relationship between subject and object, and in terms of assimilation, general schemes and accommodation, the developing child passes through a sensori-motor stage to the pre-operatory and ultimately to the concrete and formal operational stages. This type of constructivism advances in successive levels of equilibria according to certain capacities on the part of the individual to know the world around him or her. Knowing, Furth insists, is a capacity not a content. Hence the constructions of cognition do not occur at exactly the same time for each person. Yet each individual does develop according to some general patterns and within general time frameworks.

Extending out from the center of our epistemological wheel, we travel along a spoke which articulates the relationships between structure and order. This process which I shall call 'de-centering' — assuming a term which is already in Piaget and which recurs throughout this volume — links Piaget's work with that of Michel Foucault. Charles Scott, whose own work is more closely associated with that of Martin Heidegger and Medard Boss, sets both Piaget and Foucault together at a point along the cir-cumference of our wheel. Scott's concern is philosophical; we need not label it more specifically phenomenological. He seeks to elaborate the form of human self-understanding in terms of certain regions of opposing occur-rences. He is not as specific about these oppositions as Furth is about the binary relations that underlie human development. But then Scott's task is of a different sort. He takes notions such as opposition, event and region and demonstrates their presence within reality. Thus the event of an op-position establishes a discontinuity between one historical frame and another. Order is formed in the relationship between structure and history. Structure is established in the discontinuities which make order possible. The region in which structure can arise maps out the non-opposition of opposing occurrences. Hence Scott argues that order means disorder, since structure means discontinuity. He finds this same condition in both Piaget and Foucault. Despite Piaget's severe doubts (in his little book on structuralism) about Foucault's enterprise, Scott points out the non-opposition present in this conflict.

Returning again to the center of the wheel, a group of about twenty people gathered together to discuss the concept of structure in Piaget's genetic psychology. Donn Welton, whose work on language and percep-tion in Edmund Husserl has led him to a consideration of Piaget, sets forth the problematic for the Faculty Seminar. He identifies some central definitions of structure in relation to the idea of genesis in Piaget's writings. He focusses on structure as a whole system of self-regulating transformations. Wholeness, transformation, and self-regulation — these are the three concepts which Piaget, in *Introduction to Structuralism,* identifies as characteristic of a wide variety of structuralisms — including his own. The irreversible ordering, which Scott also develops, is self-regulating. At each stage, a wholeness is formed. The transformation is that which is necessary to bring about a new wholeness. Genetically, transformations are irreversible, but structurally they are reversible, allowing for the possibility of comparing the different equilibrated totalities.

The Faculty Seminar maintains its attention quite specifically on the interpretation of Piagetian concepts. Discussion however is not devoid of criticism, for the group is composed of psychologists, philosophers, physicists, literary critics and sociologists at Stony Brook and nearby universities in addition to the conference speakers. Delineating a web of relationships between notions such as subjective dissatisfaction, psychological logic, equilibrium, epistemic subject, structures of experience and topological spaces, the group brings considerable light to the achievements and limitations of the Piagetian corpus. Given the topic, however, principal attention is given to the theoretical and practical implications of Piaget's work in the past twenty years or so, that is, since he began articulating his approach in terms of structuralist thinking. Though his basic epistemological scheme has not changed, the way he presents it has been modified since his first publication in 1907 (at the age of eleven). The reader should therefore be aware that the Faculty Seminar group is directed more specifically to the later writings.

With the Faculty Seminar serving as an appropriate reformation of a nucleus, Edward Casey's paper takes the spotlight along a different spoke from that offered by Scott in connection with Foucault (and implicitly Heidegger). Casey provides a detailed, point-by-point comparison of Piaget's views on memory with those held by Freud. Casey notes Piaget's brief and early interest in psychoanalysis, but the subsequent departure again in terms of genetic epistemology. Yet if one turns to Freud's treatment of childhood memory, as exemplified in the case of the Wolf-man, some interesting parallels and differences can be identified. In this respect Casey brings to the study of Piaget his own ongoing interest in psychoanalysis and his current work on memory. Casey points specifically to the "transformative organization" which is present in both theories: on the one hand psychosexuality advances in stages (oral, anal and genital), on the other, intelligence follows a fourfold succession (sensori-motor, preoperatory, concrete operational and formal operational intelligence). In Freud, the memory of a childhood experience has its parallel in the affective schemes which Piaget reinterprets according to the intelligence of later developmental stages.

Movement along an additional spoke of the wheel takes the reader in the
direction of Adorno and the Frankfurt Institute for Social Research. The
introduction of critical theory provides a perspective which Piaget himself
does not entertain but which is nevertheless crucial for a full understanding of Piaget's enterprise. Susan Buck-Morss recalls a previous study in
which she demonstrates that Piaget has made "an epistemological mistake"
in claiming universality of formal operations. Despite Piaget's attempts to
apply his theory and experiments to other cultures, Buck-Morss argues
that formal-mathematical operations are not achieved by individuals
within many non-Western cultures. Thus she argues for a de-centering of
consciousness into the material world. She applies Piaget's term "decentering" to Adorno's notion of the observer as part of the process under
description and therefore conditioned by the social and material conditions of the examining process. Centers shift. Thus when Buck-Morss
writes that "second nature isn't very natural," she means that what Piaget
takes as rooted in the basic structures of intelligence is nevertheless conditioned by social reality, and social realities alter from culture to culture.
Social and cultural contradictions are overcome by myths which provide
logical models for interpersonal interaction. Such myths also tend to cover
up the social function of these contradictions. Yet present within fairy tales
or images of the trickster, certain paradigms for a particular society are incorporated and reiterated but without explicitly demonstrating the forms
of oppression which are present even in language itself. Thus Buck-Morss
calls for concentration on dialectical, cognitive operations rather than
abstract, formal operations. Only in this way can the forms of oppression
present in seemingly harmless fairy tales be brought to light. Attention to
dialectical, cognitive operations might, Buck-Morss suggests, lead to the
utopian possibilities of renaming the world in terms of dialectical skills and
their enactment in society.

Curiously, it is also the question of language which William Richardson
explores in connection with Jacques Lacan's structural psychoanalysis.
Piaget groups Lacan along with the linguistic structuralists because of
Lacan's thesis that the symptoms of the unconscious are present in the
language of the self. Buck-Morss' consideration of the role of language is to
demonstrate how it can be abused in the name of universality in order to
cover up certain social contradictions. Richardson introduces Lacan in
order to show that language is the place in which the self is most fully articulated and certainly the only place in which an understanding of the patient's unconscious drives is possible. Richardson, as a psychoanalyst and
an authority on Heidegger, is led to consider Piaget's interest in the sym-

bolic function of the child. This symbolic function, which is most precisely identified in the spoken words formed by the child, involves a rendering present through words what is, in fact, absent. The parallel between the introduction of symbolization at the pre-operatory stage according to Piaget and the move to the symbolic order after what Lacan calls the "mirror phase" demonstrates a similarity in their thinking. In both cases, the function of symbolization occurs quite early in the development of the individual. But also symbolization is identified as a critical feature of the child's development. For Lacan, the symbolic order represents the affirmation by the child of the *nom-du-père,* which counts as both the father's name and father's negation of the child's activities. When the child understands that the father has what the mother desires (i.e., the phallus) and when the father exerts this authority in giving the child his name and his prohibitions, the child has acquired the possibility of symbolization. Similarly when the child is able to go beyond sensori-motor recognition of shapes and objects which he or she assimilates and to which he or she accommodates, then, in Piaget's model, symbolization begins and subsequent linguistic operations become possible. By focussing on words and language, Richardson finds that Lacan gives a locus to the universal laws which regulate the unconscious activities of the mind. In both the case of Lacan and Piaget, the epistemic subject (which was much debated in the Faculty Seminar) is de-ego-centered (as Richardson puts it) or is ex-centric (as Lacan names it). The epistemic subject is therefore a linguistic, or more specifically, speaking subject. Here Richardson reintroduces what was subterranean in Scott's paper: the Heideggerian notion of Dasein. Dasein, Richardson says, is an ex-centric, de-centered self. The Being of beings, in which Dasein situates itself, is the place where the *Logos* (word, language, logic, structure, Christ) speaks. Language speaks man. Man is spoken by the symbols which enter into human growth at the initial stages of development. This holds for both Lacan and Piaget.

Hence the circumference of the wheel has been delineated by the different spokes which are the spokesmen of the Piagetian enterprise — even into domains where Piaget himself does not operate. Yet the wheel could not turn without a hub, and for the collection of papers and discussion that follow, Piaget's thought constitutes an excellent point of departure and point of return. His recent concerns with interdisciplinary study and the place of the human sciences serve as the implicit call for an inquiry such as the one we offer here. By decentering his thought into the formulations of Foucault, Freud, Adorno, Lacan and Heidegger, many of the dimensions of the human sciences as we know them today are brought into play and given a voice. It is only fitting that this voice now be given an opportunity to speak in its own words.

PIAGET'S THEORY OF KNOWLEDGE

Hans G. Furth

Piaget asked a philosopher's question on the nature of human knowledge.[1] He investigated it, however, as a biological scientist, observing knowledge as living and growing in the child. His claim to originality is to have turned a philosophical epistemology into a scientific one.

Knowledge is taken in its broadest possible sense and potentially includes any reciprocal contact between an organism and an event through which this event becomes something known by the organism. As a living dialectical relation between knower and known, Piaget described knowledge in terms of three basic concepts: (1) assimilation, the ingoing process of adopting data; (2) general schemes, the organism's internal capacity to assimilate; and (3) accommodation, the outgoing process of applying general schemes to partaicular contents. These are three conceptual perspectives of the one phenomenon, namely, knowledge in all its various stages.

The two main stages of knowledge are: (1) instinctual; and (2) developmental, with a further subdivision of (2) into: (a) sensori-motor; and (b) conceptual. In its extreme or ideal form, instinctual knowledge is built by evolution into the physiology of the organism whereas developmental knowledge requires lived experience through which the individual organism constructs this knowledge. 2(a) comprises the know-how of external actions, 2(b) the know-how of internal thinking. The internal capacity—also called schemes or cognitive structures—is the biological instrument of assimilation. It is conceived as an organ of knowledge and determines its particular stage: an instinctual structure underlies instinctual behavior and similarly with sensori-motor and conceptual behavior.

1

Piaget proposed that knowledge in the broad sense is one main component of a person's psychology, while the other component is affect.[2] Knowledge coordinates the content of psychological life; affect provides the dynamic motor force (motivation, value) to do one thing rather than something else. Both components are present in any one behavior. Knowledge itself can become an affective force, particularly in humans in whom by its own functioning it is self-expansive. Knowledge, as a psychological function, is predicated on the organism as a whole. It is the person who has capacities and corresponding knowledge, while the knowledge underlying part-systems (for example, digestion) belongs to the physiology, not the psychology of a person. For this reason Piaget limits the meaning of "maturation" to physiological growth and contrasts it with the psychological growth which he calls "development."

Why does Piaget use the concept of knowledge so broadly? First, to point out that a knowledge component (with its corresponding internal structure, assimilation and accommodation) is present in any vital functioning, but primarily to stress the continuity between action knowledge and conceptual knowledge. While philosophers have tended to limit the meaning of knowledge to conceptual, usually verbalized and verifiable, knowledge and proposed highly relevant distinctions for this, they have tended to forget that conceptual knowledge is merely the relative end-product of an evolutionary and developmental process and has many communalities with less advanced forms of behavior. Piaget started with the assumption that in all behavior there is some underlying knowledge. In knowledge one can distinguish form and content. Content derives from the particular event to which knowledge is directed, whereas form derives from the internal structure. Content is often observable; form, as such, never. Equivalent words for form are "general framework," "structure," "meaning," "understanding," and "essence;" equivalent words for content are "fact," "information," and "stimulus." At the sensori-motor stage Piaget's favorite term for internal structures is "schemes" or "coordinations of action;" schemes at the conceptual stage are "operations" or "pre-operations." The totality of a person's available schemes is this person's intelligence. Piaget is concerned with knowledge as a general capacity, hence with intelligence, not with knowledge of particular content. For most people, the concept of intelligence evokes the individual differences of normative IQ scores. For Piaget, however, the stress is on what is common and characteristic of all humans as they grow from infancy to adulthood.

This growth is called development. It is a process different from physiological maturation but different also from mere accumulation of new knowledge content which can be called learning from outside (related to accommodation). Rather development is a constructing on the part of the child, that is, from within. It is a progressive restructuring and results in the child's acquisition of new knowledge capacities. Piaget speaks of different stages in development which reflect differences in structure. For Piaget development is intrinsic to knowledge. From this fundamental identity—development is but intelligence in the making—flows the theory's justification for its claim to be scientific and not merely philosophical. For what is unobservable in itself, becomes observable in its changing during the child's life and therefore amenable to controlled observation.

On the question of "innate" versus "learned," Piaget rejects both extremes, since development by definition requires individual experience but at the same time it is not a learning of outside content. In fact Piaget's constructivist position is quite radical and knows no absolute beginning or end. There is no rock bottom knowledge datum which comes from outside and on which the child builds. Rather at the very lowest level the infant is already biologically equipped with internal schemes which give structure to what becomes a "known" content. The growth of these schemes is the development of intelligence. The scheme as an instrument of assimilation is always the primary fact in Piaget's viewpoint.

The infant's first development takes place in the *sensori-motor* period, at a time when there is no conceptual knowledge; rather knowledge is undifferentiated from action or even more precisely the child does not differentiate between self as the subject of the action, the action and the object of the action. The infant lives at a level of practical know-how and develops increasingly integrated coordinations of actions. Piaget described meticulously his own three children's behavior in the context of confronting little problems.[3] The key concept is goal-directed activity in the form of means-end relations in which an observer can interpret the beginning of human intelligence. This includes sense and body coordination for perception, spatial coordinations for moving around in space, learning of new content and of signals and retention in the form of recognition.

For example, consider a six-month old baby beginning to crawl. Insofar as knowledge is concerned there is, first of all, some sort of body coordination. Crawling implies spatial knowledge. The child knows how to get from here to there. This child, with his crawling scheme, finds himself or herself in a particular spatial situation, for instance, wanting to get from here to the table. In terms of this particular model, the child will assimilate the situation to his or her crawling scheme, to his or her spatial knowledge. In other words, the child will construct and coordinate the input so that it gives him or her cues on how to crawl. Accommodation takes place when the child pays attention to these cues and applies his or her general spatial knowledge to this particular event. Every event is particular; every event has some element of newness, even if it is a subjective newness such that the child is a different subject one second later. There is always assimilation and accommodation. Accommodation means that knowledge is there to be used. Schemes are not objects of knowledge. Schemes are capacities to use knowledge in certain events. This is sensori-motor knowledge. The child acquires sensori-motor knowledge by experiencing the environment, and by experiencing it intelligently. Intelligence is another word for the totality of schemes.

Sensori-motor intelligence is very intelligent. It can have means-end relations; it can be goal-directed; and one can have a sensori-motor intention. A person with sensori-motor intelligence can learn new content. As the child moves around in a room, the child will quickly learn that there is a table there, the first time the child knocks against it. The next time he moves more smoothly and efficiently. The child has learned that there is a table in the room by means of sensori-motor memory, recognition memory, as distinguished from recall memory. The child recognizes something that is present and benefits from past experience.

The separation of subject, action and object is a gradual process which Piaget observed in the infant's search for a hidden object. Initially infants behave literally as if their actions produce objects and the cessation of action engenders their annihilation. Eventually this behavior changes and the search for objects becomes systematic to the point that one can unequivocally assert that infants know things exist independently of their own present action. This knowledge is nothing other than the first glimmer of conceptual knowing, for now things are not merely things-of-action but are beginning to be objects-of-knowing, in other words, concepts. This transition, occurring at about eighteen months, must not be conceived as a sudden change from night to day; on the contrary it takes another five or more years before concepts become logically stable.

Object formation ushers in the *pre-operatory* period during which children slowly construct the stable categories of knowing characteristic of adult thinking. Just as he inferred the emergence of the object concept from empirical evidence, namely a critical point in the child's search for a hidden object, Piaget inferred the concomitant symbolic capacity from children's external gestures.[4] Sensori-motor functioning is limited to signals which are associated with present situations or bodily states; in contrast, symbols follow from object formation in that they, like the objects, are separated from the present thing and re-present a known but absent object. In Piaget's terminology symbols and representations are the same thing. They are at first external, such as in symbolic play. Moreover, Piaget suggests that what we identify and experience as a mental image is essentially an internalized and diminutive representation. Note how all this goes contrary to the assumed primacy of the object as a stimulus and of internal representation as the medium of knowledge. In Piaget's theory, object formation is the end product of early sensori-motor development, and internal representation waits upon object formation. It follows from this that symbols are dependent on post-sensori-motor knowledge and not vice versa. Language, as the symbolic system for society's communication, is one variety of the symbolic function. Piaget is perhaps the only serious investigator of knowledge who was able to separate conceptual thinking from language and propose that language — however important its function for other purposes — is neither sufficient nor necessary for intellectual development. My own studies[5] on profoundly deaf persons provided a strong confirmation of this revolutionary position. Another consequence of object and symbol formation is the capacity for memory recall which, in contrast to recognition, requires a symbol.

These newly acquired capacities provide the child with a formidable task and challenge. Being able to separate thing from object and to think of it in its absence takes the security of practical functioning away from children and makes them live in a symbolic world of their own construction. Before this, not only were action and object undifferentiated, but also affect and action went together. But now as knowledge comes into its own, there occurs the separation of knowledge and affect. The awareness of self with its subsequent consciousness is another consequence of this developmental watershed. Piaget described the pre-operatory thinking of children as immersed at first in a self-centered perspective which is constantly reinforced by their fantasy.[6] Their thinking becomes de-centered and "objective" in proportion to their construction of a framework of concepts. Piaget calls these general concepts "operations."

Operations are the overriding logical categories through which the world appears as stable and consistent: hierarchical classification, serial ordering, and numerical quantification are major examples of logically self-consistent and closed systems. Once achieved they enable the child to move from one point within the system to another, based on the system's internal logic. This is what Piaget means by reversibility and conservation: the system remains stable throughout its possible transformations. Thus children around seven years of age begin to understand that: (1) given B

and B' as subclasses of A, there are more instances of A than of B'; or (2) given $A + B = C$, then $C - A = B$; or (3) if A is bigger than B and B is bigger than C, it follows that A is bigger than C. For the child's experience this understanding is based on an internal criterion. In other words, in the above examples the answers are not empirical facts to be remembered but are true because they are part of the system. As such they must be true and cannot be proven false by experience. These operations are applied in a great variety of ways to the basic physical and social categories that make up the known reality of the adult person: physical causality, inter-personal relations, intentionality,[7] historical time, etc.

Piaget proposed two stages of operations: concrete operations which are elaborated between seven and twelve years old and formal operations beginning around twelve years old.[8] Concrete operations were illustrated above and are called concrete because even though in themselves they are theoretical structures their contents are concrete events (present or concretely imaginable). In contrast, formal operations are even further removed from concrete instances and directly bear on logical propositions or hypothetical possibilities. Formal operations are used in the thinking that makes scientific experimentation and logical-mathematical theorizing possible. While the universal distribution of concrete operations across all healthy adults and societies is pretty well established, this is not so for formal operations. Even in our own culture many adults do not seem to use formal operations. Generally the acquisition of formal, much more than concrete, operations is sensitive to a specifically motivating environment, such as an occupational specialty. If with Piaget one holds to a dynamic view of intelligence with knowledge functioning simultaneously at different levels and no uniform developmental advance in all areas, one understands why for him it is concepts and not children who are in stages and why one cannot expect to discover reliable and standardized age norms comparable to IQ performances.

It would be inappropriate to say of these operations that they are retained in memory; they are not things to remember, but structures that belong to the person. In a real sense they make what the person is and conserve themselves by their own functioning. Neither should one think of operations as things that a person knows: they are not objects to be known, rather they are structures to be used in their various applications. This is not to say that one cannot reflect on them and make them conscious objects of knowing; but basically they are a capacity to do something, a know-how to coordinate, relate, anticipate, and solve problems, not practically like sensori-motor schemes, but internally and conceptually. In themselves they are unconscious.

The entire biological system of knowing — of making adaptive contact with the environment — is subject to its own intrinsic principles of self-regulation for which Piaget knows no better word than *equilibration*.[9] The various manifestations of knowing as touched upon above participate in this all-encompassing principle and reflect it in its dialectic terms, such as assimilation-accommodation or subject-object. This concept is crucial if one asks the obvious question as to what brings about intellectual development. If any present functioning of the knowing system is characterized by a self-regulatory balance, what is it that disturbs this balance and moves it in the direction of progress? If one looks for the answer outside the system — environmental events, physiological states — one violates the self-regulatory principle and knowledge becomes the organism's copy of the empirical world. This indeed is the viewpoint of empiricistic epistemology and it underlies a wide-spread misunderstanding of Piaget's terminology in which the concept of assimilation is deformed to mean habitual knowledge, and accommodation the construction of new knowledge.

Now, accommodation does have something to do with new knowledge since by definition it is the application of general schemes to a particular content. Every instance has some elements of newness; no two contingencies are exactly alike. As you attend to the following information "9 August 1896" the new accommodation to this particular date seems more important than its assimilation to schemes of reading, language and concepts of historical time, etc. which by now are well established within you. If you are motivated to remember this information as Piaget's birthday, it would seem that accommodation is in fact the source of new knowledge. However, when we say this we neglect two crucial conditions. First, there is assimilation to presently available schemes of knowing without which there would be no information at all. You may not be conscious of and you certainly do not remember how you acquired these schemes. Second, what is acquired is new content, but not a new knowing capacity. Piaget's theory is, however, primarily concerned with knowing as a capacity, not as particular content, and development (and evolution) invariably deals with general capacity. Hence, accommodation does not at all suffice to explain development.

To illustrate how Piaget uses the principle of equilibration as the primary internal cause of structural development, take a young girl playing a record player.[10] To start with there is the most immediate and external reaction of the subject (who in this case has already acquired sensori-motor and post-sensori-motor schemes) to the object. She uses the object according to its obvious function, that is, she assimilates the object to available schemes and takes note (or becomes conscious) of the superficial result of the action, that is, she accommodates schemes to the particular contingencies. Gradually the child moves from the periphery of observation to the center in a two-fold manner: she constructs and becomes aware of the internal regulatory coordinations of her own actions and at the same time of the intrinsic mechanisms of the object. Fig. 1 is from a recent monograph and depicts the equilibration between subject (S) and object (O) and between observable "facts" (Obs.) and inferred coordinations (Coord.). Coord. S are the subject's general schemes which, once developed, make up the subject's intelligence. If one calls Obs. O the initial "facts," the diagram illustrates how Coord. S structures these facts into "objective" knowledge through which the observables are now different from what they were when the process started. These new observables, however, lead to a renewed progression and so the spiral of knowing continues *ad infinitum.*

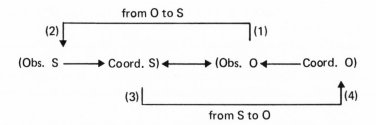

Fig. I. Model of equilibration: S = subject, O = object, Obs. = observable 'facts,' Coord. = inferred coordination of Obs. The principle tendencies of knowing move from (I) to (4) and back to (I) in an open-ended spiral.

To answer finally the question as to the source of development: this is to be found within the workings of knowledge itself. Since knowing means constructing, and constructing constantly creates new perspectives, these perspectives lead to a dialectical conflict with previous views and thereby instigate a new compensatory synthesis. In simpler terms, while assimilation and accommodation are the twin processes of any knowing, they are the obligatory occasions for further development insofar as present activity feeds back into the subject's structure. See Fig. 2.

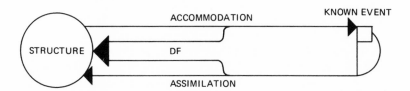

Fig. 2. Developmental feedback (DF) as source of structural growth.

The *implications* of Piaget's theory extend as far as human knowledge and its subjects, particularly children. It presents knowledge not as something imposed on humans by heredity or environment, but as freely created from within—freedom is always relative to the nature of the subject. It therefore provides a basis for a humane and relevant perspective on the person and indicates respect for personal freedom and individual variability beyond fixed norms, reasonable emotional control and intelligent social concern. It recognizes the tremendous dangers and pitfalls inherent in the very fact of objective and symbolic differentiation and appreciates the years of active development it takes to reach a tolerably mature and always relative objectivity. Nevertheless, this capacity to construct and reconstruct is at the same time one of man's most valuable functions which in its own way can be used constructively in fields other than physical knowing. Interpersonal and emotional maturity, ideals, art, and music, all participate in this intelligence. An artificial split between them and knowledge is baneful for both sides. If you have ever observed a child's excitement over an intellectual insight it is obvious that intellectual health is a most powerful and ego-positive component of overall mental health which in educational or clinical practice we neglect to the detriment of the children. However, to know what activities are conducive to intellectual health requires an explicit theory of knowledge—this is possibly the most practical application of Piaget's theory.[11]

References

1 Jean Piaget, *Insights and Illusions of Philosophy*, trans. Wolfe Mays (New York: World, 1971). Originally published in 1965.

2 Jean Piaget and B. Inhelder, *Psychology of the Child*, trans. Helen Weaver (New York: Basic Books, 1969). Originally published in 1966.

3 Jean Piaget, *The Origins of Intelligence in Children,* trans. Margaret Cook (New York: Norton, 1963). Originally published in 1936.

4 Jean Piaget, *Play, Dreams and Imitations in Childhood,* trans. C. Gattegno and F.M. Hodgson (New York: Norton, 1962). Originally published in 1946.

5 Hans G. Furth, *Thinking Without Language: Psychological Implications of Deafness* (New York: Free Press, 1966), and *Deafness and Learning* (Belmont, California: Wadsworth, 1973).

6 Jean Piaget, *The Child's Conception of the World,* trans. Joan and Andrew Tomlinson (New York: Humanities Press, 1969). Originally published in 1926.

7 Jean Piaget, *The Moral Judgment of the Child,* trans. Marjorie Gabain (New York: Free Press, 1965). Originally published in 1932.

8 Jean Piaget and B. Inhelder, *Psychology of the Child, op. cit.*

9 Jean Piaget, *Biology and Knowledge,* trans. Beatrix Walsh (Chicago: University of Chicago Press, 1971). Originally published in 1967.

10 Jean Piaget, *The Grasp of Consciousness: Action and Concept in the Young Child,* trans. Susan Wedgwood (Cambridge: Harvard University Press, 1976). Originally published in 1974.

11 Hans G. Furth, *Piaget for Teachers* (Engelwood Cliffs, New Jersey: Prentice-Hall, 1970).

Discussion

Question₁: When a light is associated with food, the light becomes part of the food scheme, part of the sensori-motor scheme. The light is associated with food behavior. Doesn't this behavior involve some stimulus?

Hans Furth: The stimulus is what we call the light or the signal for food. But a mouse sees light and assimilates it to the eating scheme.

Question₁: In other words you would not want to interpret a signal as instilling recall?

Furth: No. Perceptual cues can be called signals. We never see a whole thing. We focus on certain aspects, but they are signals for the whole. Signal behavior is called sensori-motor behavior.

Fred Levine: What is the role of neurological development in Piaget's system? How does it interact with experience in the development of intelligence?

Furth: Neurological development falls under maturation. It is not psychology. Piaget knows it takes place. It is vital and we cannot exist without it. By itself, it is not psychology. And Piaget has nothing to say about it. It is quite possible that, together with the development of physiological changes, the maturation of the nervous system could be responsible for intelligence. Piaget has no objection to that at all. But Piaget does not think that you can simply say that a child develops operational thinking because the nervous system has evolved to a particular point. Piaget does not physiologize; and when Piaget talks of schemes or structures, these are psychological structures, not physiological structures.

Dick Howard: I am worried about the objects. You were very careful to point out to us how Piaget does not want to fall into the trap of identifying isolated objects. You want to pose the problem of the object. But throughout your first example of the baby crawling to something, why does the child pick this or that goal? When your little girl is playing the record player what is, in fact, the object? There seems to be no role for fantasy or desire. You or Piaget seem to be imposing a certain adult, logical means-end rationality onto the child or learning person.

Furth: You are quite right in pointing out that Piaget has left out a huge facet of psychology, namely, everything that goes with motivation, affects, etc. He knows that. He only deals with formation. Piaget has no answer as to why a child plays with this paper rather than this pencil. Fantasy is nothing but making objects present which are absent. The child lives in a fantasy world. A two or three year old child has just acquired the capacity to symbolize, and he symbolizes life wildly. He is completely confused by it. The whole pre-operative child lives in fantasy.

Howard: The point was that if one does not neglect motive, affect, desire and the rest, and if it is the case that those are nonetheless operative in the child whom one is observing, then might it not be the case that what we describe the child as doing is not at all what the child is doing. The child may be reconstructing some fantasmatic world of its own. On account of that we would be imposing our adult logic or our adult world onto the child.

Furth: I think your point is well taken, but if you read Piaget's observations you would find that he is a very good psychologist. In the final analysis everything is inference. There is always the danger that we impose our motivational goals on the child, but I think Piaget is careful enough to escape that error. Obviously however he is not infallible.

Peter Dollard: You distinguish between humans and other higher animals. It seems to me that animals problem solve in new situations. They also evidence conceptualization in a great number of ways.

Furth: They problem solve, but I don't think that they conceptualize.

Question₂: What brings the child from sensori-motor behavior up to the perceptual level? Is there a different sort of equilibrium needed to require the child to have complete object permanence?

Furth: Piaget would answer that the knowledge process in itself brings about a post-sensori-motor stage, because you already have subject/object distinctions.

Question₂: Why does it continue from sensori-motor development? What finally makes this sort of discontinuity different as an approach to development?

Furth: It isn't as discontinuous as you might expect. As soon as you think of means-ends relations, you have a subject and an object: a subject who wants to reach a certain object. All it means is that the object is known better itself. Piaget describes very carefully how the search for the hidden object takes on more and more conceptual and continuous characteristics. It is a very gradual process. Within the sensori-motor process different stages of functioning lead more and more to what we eventually call conceptual understanding. The beginnings of conceptual understanding are hardly perceptible. With regard to a three year old child, he or she may have some conceptual understanding but still primarily a sensori-motor functioning. For example, language in itself is a symbol. A child first uses it only in the presence of events. There is no radical discontinuity. Quite the opposite. The object concept, properly speaking, is really only a development of the child's first operation. It takes five years to develop. You cannot say that there is any sudden jump from one level to another.

Robert Ray: Does Piaget allow for instinctual-affective behavior? Let me give you an example to show you what I mean. I'm not sure that this has actually happened but perhaps something like it has. Birds will sing if they hear their call once and can develop very complicated calls upon hearing it once. The explanation is that they have the capacity built into them, but to trigger that capacity they have to hear the song.

Furth: True. There are all kinds of instinctual behavior.

Ray: In that case, the instinct needed the experience.

Furth: Yes. But for Piaget, there is no sudden jump from instinctual to developmental behavior. Rather there are all kinds of intermediaries on all different levels.

Question₃: I would like to go back and, in relation to the dialectic, set a framework in which to discuss Piaget. From my own views of Piaget it seems that he presents us with an ideal dialectic in the sense that the situation more or less predetermines subjectivity. There is no visible subjectivity. The child's concept of self is basically an environmental presence.

Question4: I think a lot of us are having trouble understanding your distinctions between conceptual and verbal knowledge. I have a couple of questions related to this. In the question earlier about recall, how does Piaget handle the problem of production deficiency in the infant and in other animals? Also, what I find very curious about your descriptions is the assumption that what an organism wants in the future is not conceptual knowledge. Wanting a banana is not the same thing as remembering a banana. What makes the future different from the past in that respect? In both cases, the banana is not there.

Furth: The organism experiences itself as wanting a banana. It can be quite sure of wanting the object without conceptualizing it. It is the same as sex. You can feel the want without conceptualizing it. You don't have to conceptualize it for the banana to be there. The child is hungry or cold. Does he have to have the concept of hunger before crying? Or does the child have to have the concept of cold before wanting to feel warm?

Question4: I think he has to have the concept of banana before he can want a banana. Is not the "banana" a concept?

Francis Palmer: I think the problem rests in taking the symbol for the banana. The question is why isn't the symbol the banana, if Piaget uses it to obtain conceptualization?

Furth: I distinguish symbol from signal. If a dog is locked in a room, he wants to get out. In the lab, we make some movements. I close the door. Now is that a signal or a symbol? Clearly the dog tells me that he wants to get out. Does the dog have the concept of "exit?" For an outsider to observe conceptually, you have to have evidence that the person can reconstruct or recall an absent event. It has to be absent either as an event or absent as a present need. A present need doesn't require conceptualization. Do you really think that if a child is cold and wants to feel warm that a child has to have the concept of warmth?

Question4: I don't think that is a parallel example.

Furth: The child is hungry and wants a banana. It's the same thing. The only difference is that the child has learned a specific food. But why the specific food? Because there is no other sensori-motor discrimination — just like the dog who wants to get out. We have two exits, but perhaps the dog will soon learn that it is much more fun or much better to get out of one exit rather than the other. That is discrimination, not conceptualization.

Robin Alsop: But what about when my dog brings the ball over to me and I take it in my hand and the dog sits there and waits to play fetch. Is that conceptualization?

Furth: No! That is sensori-motor behavior. The dog knows that you are playing with him. He indicates this to you by giving you a sign. That's what a signal is.

Alsop: But you said it would be symbolization if the animal were to say "Yesterday, I had a good banana." Isn't my dog saying that yesterday he played a good game of ball?

Furth: No, because the dog merely wants to play with you now. If the dog told me that yesterday he had a good game, that would be symbolization. I'm not convincing you. But what are these interpretations anyhow? They are interpretations according to a theory. Every behavior has to be interpreted or assimilated according to a theory.

Edward S. Casey: I have one question of clarification and one substantive question. I thought that equilibration applied to a structure not to the relation between objects as in coordinated action. I was curious about your use of the term.

Furth: I started off saying that the subject and the object are simply conceptual distinctions. When we talk about structure, it includes everything. When I identify you as a person, I am applying my structure of what I know that a person is to you. You have not become an object of that structure. You are part of the structure.

Casey: But you include on your diagram the objects as at least an observable. It seems to me that that is a different object from the object of the structure.

Furth: It is only different because the structure has separated it. Insofar as you are part of this equilibrated structure, I know you as a person.

Casey: In other words, by the time we reach equilibration we are beyond the observable level.

Furth: Oh, it is observable in terms of subjective experience. In terms of what is observable to you.

Casey: Okay. And this is my further question. Is it the case that we always accommodate? For Piaget, we accommodate to particular events. It is surely possible to accommodate to a type of event and not to a particular event. I can accommodate, for example, to what I would call crowd behavior without accommodating to a particular crowd. Now is that genuine accommodation, and if so what kind of accommodation is it?

Furth: Accommodation that is usually accompanied by symbolic behavior. That is why we accommodate to a particular symbol that symbolizes a particular concept—whether it is in language or whether you express it in language . . .

Casey: So the particular has passed from perceivable object onto a symbol, a word, or some other concretum? He would end with the paradox of a particular type. It is hard to imagine a particular type since types are general by nature.

Furth: That is where symbols and language come in. You accommodate to the symbolic expression that stands for your thinking.

Casey: So actually it's the expression of a type and not the type itself.

Josef Nivnik: As far as I know Piaget is much more popular among psychologists than among philosophers despite the fact that epistemology was always philosophical and despite the fact, as you said, that he is against anyone calling him a psychologist. What would you say in connection with this? I think that this is due to an arbitrariness in his notions of knowledge and epistemology. From what I have understood, he just describes the process of adaptation, or adaptive mechanisms, or the development of child intelligence. These concerns are already named in psychology, which is more precise than epistemology or knowledge. I would say that this is all very confusing for philosophers also.

Furth: Piaget considers himself a Kantian. He believes in the Kantian *a priori*. However, it is not an historical *a priori*. *A priori* categories stand at the end of development. Of course it is paradoxical. On the other hand, Piaget talks about the foundation of mathematics and about what mathematics is. That's what philosophers talk about. So what he's saying obviously has some relevance to philosophers too.

Nivnik: The basic relevance is that this is called epistemology, not science.

Furth: You are quite right. Piaget would like to be recognized by philosophers and yet he finds himself recognized by psychologists.

STRUCTURE AND ORDER

Charles E. Scott

1 The Issue of Order in Structuralism

The subject of this discussion is the form of human self-understanding. The issue to be addressed is how we are to understand the orders which provide our sense of unity or sameness in the midst of experiential diversity. The question is how are we to interpret the historical nature of order as we reflect the order in which we find ourselves. I shall make reference, as we proceed, to Foucault and Piaget, whose work, in their striking differences, allows us to focus a major issue: can experimental data, by virtue of its accuracy, tend to destroy the order which forms its basis? I understand that question, in our context, to refer to the relation of history and "data." Behind this question and reflected in it will be another question: how are we to understand human intelligence? By putting together our subject, issue, question and focus, we may ask: how are we interpretively to order the given structure of awareness in a manner of intelligence that reflects immediately the occurrence of its own historicity? The conviction which I shall elaborate in the course of my observations is that human imaginativeness and energy depend on how we reflect the uncertainty and possibility which indwell (or constitute) all aspects of structure and order. *Historicity* names the inevitability of partiality, and hence of uncertainty and possibility, in any occurrence of unity. If a complex event of human awareness does not reflect its own historicity, it immediately refuses the meaning of its own partiality and a major aspect of its capacity for renewal and self-change.

I feel paradoxical as I say that energy and form are intimately related.

16

That classical insight, so much a part of our reflective tradition, is obvious. But it is also nearly forgotten in modern science and social science and is deeply in question for our culture generally. The original notion, which founded the intimacy of form and energy, lacked immediate reference to its own history and made serenely universal claims. Destiny was either the work of Fate, Chaos' granddaughter, whom even Zeus could not control, or it was the working out of directions under the control of Zeus' daughters or another deity. In both the Platonic and Aristotelian traditions, history always referred to reality or realities that stood outside of history. Our modern discovery of history and relativity, in association with the incalculable power of a cultural sense of unalterable atomistic division, means that we find difficulties with all thinking that is self-reflective in its historicity. The advent and development of the notions of history and individuality have thus threatened the meaning of form and energy, in their intimacy, for our self-understanding. In discovering history we have tended to lose the notion of sameness, because of its non-historical connotation in our civilization. We can hardly think of the historical *occurrence* of fundamental structures as a common, finite order for us all.

The emergence of concern for the structures of orders is important as an occasion for our re-inheritance of this notion of sameness. This concern for structures has picked its subject matter modestly and carefully: the structure and order of selected works of folklore or of other texts, usually isolated from more encompassing realities; the structure and order of tribal family and social relations; the structure and order of manners of speech; the structure and order of certain ways of knowing; and so forth. Within the framework of investigations of this type, one may well use principles of development, as Erickson and Piaget have, for example. In all cases, however, the issue of how structure occurs, the commonality of structure itself, is made available again with particular moment. Is biological development the common factor for intellectual order? Is formal analysis sufficient for understanding a text's structure? That is, does *form* itself name the commonality of structures? How do structures, and consequently orders, change in common? Is the possibility for change intrinsic or extrinsic vis-à-vis structures? These are not new questions, but now they are to be asked in the context of self-conscious methods of interpreting the order of texts or the human psyche. When we recall that the human mind is a linguistic, historically structured event we are prepared to see that the issues related to the structure and order of texts, language, or intelligence have to do with our nature and destiny. How we understand a method of textual interpretation or a method of interpreting human intelligence already reflects a notion of structure and order that make claims on how we are to understand our basic history and future. That means that the Greek notion of destiny and the modern notion of history are brought together, perhaps unexpectedly, in structuralist and humanistic reflection.

2 The Foundations of Orders

Stan Kenton said recently (April 9, 1977, in Nashville) that he is suspicious of the rising popularity of jazz, because in order to hear jazz "you have to have a certain perception which is unconscious, not conscious, and most people just don't have it." He had in mind, I believe, our awareness in movements, feelings, and relations of meaning which come to musical sound without words or discursive thinking. He referred to events of hearing or perception in which there is no object and no activity by that part of ourselves with which we identify ourselves and in which we know ourselves. This awareness, which Kenton said is not conscious, comes to music, and in jazz the musician is the occurrence of this awareness coming to music. He is quite outside himself when "himself" refers to a distinctive region of consciousness which is at once self-directing and aware of itself. By hearing the music and thus working with it descriptively we would be able to interpret and understand the awareness that came to music. The music would be similar to a dream that presents in itself awareness that may well not be a part of our accountable consciousness.

This depth of awareness, which according to Kenton not many of us touch in a hearing or allowing way, is a basis for what we may all hear in one way or another, viz. the tonal sounds. In that sense a founding awareness occurs as the basis for what one does and how one does it. I suspect that it is just as basic for intelligence as it is for music. I share that observation with an increasing variety of people, such as Lacan, Ricoeur, Foucault, Jung, Freud particularly in his later years, Heidegger and Boss. In the context of this observation, which people elaborate in very different ways, I want to raise the following question about the form or structure of awareness: how are structures that are basic for our awareness and hence our intelligence to be understood in relation to history?

Foucault has shown that the time of our awareness was born in relation to a changing sense of the nature of organism. In medicine, for example, biological method changed from describing the surface structures of living things in their pervasive interrelation to classifying structures internal for distinct organisms, such as skin or lungs, without an imperative to see linkage among the organisms. The biological organ or the text or the social structure tended to be seen as a self-defining thing. A consequence is that the ideas of same, whole and unity tend to refer to particular things in their separate, internal relations. How they are in common falls from focus. The tendency is toward a monadology without a significant notion of pre-established harmony.

We see the institutional outcropping of this enormous change in pre-discursive awareness in the specialization of knowledge. Not only is medicine a radically separate field from, say, literary criticism, but within medicine itself, specialization has developed by reference to separate organs, and the separation of the organs is further underscored in the difficulty of discourse among specialists.

This notion of our time — the separate autonomy of physical and non-physical organisms — is often lived in the paradox that human beings seem to be a common linkage for medicine, linguistics, philosophy, economics, etc. The fundamental, intuitive sense expressed in the order of specialization appears to conflict radically and simultaneously with a dim, but present sense that we, the partial authors of the orders of separation and isolation, are in common in those separate orders. How are we to reflect our being in common in the orders common for our time?

My purpose is not to look at responses to this question about our destiny. I want, rather, to underscore that this question is a part of our destiny. It happens as a conflict in primordial awareness in which our sense of organic structure and our sense of our own being do not mean each other. As a result this aspect of our awareness reflects itself as uncertainty of human being in the certainty of perception regarding organisms and as uncertainty of that perception of organisms in our certainty of being. The "tone" that emerges from this depth awareness is a faint "sound" of non-reality, of empty, perhaps bleating, "notes" pervasive of the strident chords of epistemological certainty; or the "tone" may be one in which confusion, absence of meaning, and disrelation quietly pervade the harmonies of our common being-together. Indeed these two cacophonous forms may both happen at once. I think that Stan Kenton is right about jazz and that Foucault is right about the priority of disorder in the orders of our age.

This situation of awareness means, for example, that knowledge and the development of knowledge, certainty and the search for certainty, are central phenomena for our self-interpretation. I suppose that would be true for any period during the era of written communication and history. The particular issue for us now is that our interpretation of knowing can take place with virtually no sense for the pre-discursive foundations of

knowing. The result is that our epistemologies usually are studies of structures and processes that are taken as composing one kind of virtually self-
contained organism — call it brain or mind or reason or intelligence. And
the epistemology itself consequently does not reflect or mean a sameness or
commonality of being beyond itself. The grounds or possibility for this
isolation of knowing appears to be the dominance of classificatory perception and of singular organisms that emerged, as Foucault has shown, in
our modern history.

We may say that the ability to be contemporary epistemologists is found
in a describable, historical development, not in an isolated transcendental,
pure, or divine region, and that that historically originated ability is common to many contemporary disciplines. These disciplines, because of the
nature of their grounding, tend not to reflect self-consciously their
historical and ontological commonality in their articulated self-
understandings. That is one of the out-croppings of our modern, depth
awareness: an atomistic perception of organism that is not alert to its own
historical and common basis with other organic beings.

3 Opposition and Event

How are we to understand structure when we find that our only tenuous-
ly related interpretive orders are founded in the orders of historical depth
awareness?

An aspect of that awareness for our attention now is opposition.
Knowledge of *what* conflicts within the fabric of a language or a set of
customs will lead to an understanding of the bases for specific separations and oppositions in given lives. But our interest is in opposition as such
in the historical patterns for our lives. *Opposition* names a structural
aspect in our being aware. Our awareness begins as much in discontinuity
as it does in continuity. We have seen that illustrated in the conflict of
atomistic perceptiveness and pervasive human being. And we are generally
familiar with the expectation that a specific identity makes possible the
visibility of the opposite of that identity. Same means other. Human being
as an object of science tends to highlight human being as also and at once
not susceptible to scientific objectification. Purity of soul means the reality
of perversity. In the psychoanalytic tradition conscious means unconscious,
and the gap between the two is not bridgeable by a conscious activity, and
so forth.

The depth and meaning of opposition has gained particular moment in
the literature on madness in recent years. From such different kinds of

thinkers as Jung, N. O. Brown and Foucault, we hear that madness manifests a fundamental situation of our depth awareness. The meaning of "shadow" in Jung's thought and "double" in Foucault's thought mean in common that fundamental contrast is intrinsic in depth awareness and that madness may articulate the opposite of an oppressively established aspect of the enunciative possibilities of a given time.

This realization that fundamental difference is fundamental for order is, indeed, a structural element of the depth possibilities for ordering. It means that our self-understanding depends on our countenancing the opposite of what we establish as valid. Otherwise unity will be lost in the partiality of our accomplishment. It also means that our knowledge will constitute a profound and probably destructive kind of forgetfulness if it does not self-consciously reflect its own ignorance. It means that when our sanity does not appropriate madness, our sanity, in its separated, organic, autonomous self-confidence, will be the very insanity that it excludes. It means that truth free of contradiction and paradox is a self-destructive separation from its own basis. It means that law without aimless creativity will be radical, anarchistic arbitrariness. It means that health care turned away from death will be a carrier of death. It means that harmony without opposition will be an enemy of human peace. And all of this because fundamental difference is a structure of the occurrence of that awareness which forms the basis for possible orders and expressions. Orders, paradoxically, are founded in separation, brokenness and division, and without dealing with modes of discontinuity we shall not be able to understand the ways we put things together with order.

The prominence of opposition and conflict is partially due to the collapse of the notion of undisturbed permanence as a primary reference for interpreting finite reality. Finitude in one form or another has dominance for the meaning of order in our time, and, primarily because of Hegel and his enormous legacy, conflict and opposition have been the most noted characteristics of what at one time was called the imperfection, viz. the finiteness, of being. But with the loss of a sense for changeless permanence we have tended also to lose our sense for height and depth, for reality other than positivity, and for awareness other than discursive knowledge and common sense. Even desire tends to be relegated to the unconscious. At least part of the reason for this loss is that sameness, universality, wholeness and oneness were associated with eternity, and when eternity fell, these other notions fell with it. With Foucault we see a struggle to reinterpret the sameness of order in the history of change and opposition, minus even the hint of an Hegelian absolute. Ordering involves a shadowed establishment, a double of the dominant, in which the conflicted opposition characteristic of the very possibility for expression and meaning is articulated. An epochal, un-everlasting beginning, as oppositions in the origin of a given consciousness, works itself out in the manners, traditions, institutions and language of a time.

Another word which we should note is *event*. Foucault has little to say about the eventfulness of things. I note the word because order and structure cannot be understood well if reference is made to order and structure without regard for their manifestness, their presence. *Opposition,* we see, names a structure of order. *Event* names the occurrence of things, their happening, and in our context it means that the occurrence of things is itself to be noted when we want to understand structures and orders. Gadamer's *Truth and Method*[1] is one account of how an *event* is in its ontological structure. It transmits historically originated meaning, engenders an horizon of possibilities in fusion with other horizons of possibilities, transcends the particularity of its total contents, and so forth. For our purposes, however, I shall note only that the event of opposition speaks of how things happen, and that happening is not a structure or an order, but the sameness of whatever occurs. We shall return to the point later, as we attempt to discover the limits of the notions of structure and order for interpreting their own reality. Without a sense for the eventfulness of things, we should be bereft of a sense of being that is unlimited by any order or structure. We should thus interpret order and structure, and opposition as well, as though they did not occur as the very opposite of vacuum and absence. The coming forth of things is the place to look if we are to understand the un-thinglike, finite commonality of oppositions. But more of that later.

4 Piaget and Foucault

I would like to make the convenient assumption about Piaget and Foucault that each is accurate in a major part of his work, that each has made major contributions to our knowledge about ourselves. The issue in question for the moment is the limits of accuracy.

Piaget is interested in the growth and integration of the knowing organism. He has given a concrete basis for recognizing and nurturing the growth of the human ability to know. And with his evidence he has dispelled the belief that the human mind functions in any way other than stages of development. He has shown how this development happens as the activity of the individual knower. The knower realizes himself gradually in the activities of relating, puzzling, contrasting and so forth. He has moved decisively away from the language of static a priori, a language which was most available to him. He has understood human knowing in terms of "abilities to function" in a "self-regulating organism."[2] The knowing organism naturally seeks laws: it is, in Piaget's word, nomothetic. His scientific goal is to identify and name those laws of intelligence, which are "quantitative relations that are comparatively constant and can be expressed in the form of mathematical functions . . . (or) plain factual information . . . which can be described in everyday language or in more or less formalized language."[3] As the very laws of intelligence change, the change itself, Piaget says, will be subject to law-abiding processes that may be described in terms of other mathematical functions or plain factual information.

A central contrast between Foucault and Piaget is now visible. For Piaget the emphasis falls on the continuity of functions expressible by informational or formalized language. For Foucault the emphasis falls on that isolation expressed in Piaget's understanding of the "self-regulating organism." Temperamentally, Piaget is inclined to see law-abiding relations and Foucault is inclined to see breakage and discontinuity. But Piaget acknowledges the probability that firm and established laws of development will change, and Foucault develops a coherent language to name and describe the historical development of discontinuity.

And yet in Piaget's language and conceptuality how can we articulate the historical and fundamental awareness that is expressed in his passion to know with accuracy and consistency? How are we to develop organically in his experimental method and his understanding of law as a self-reflection of the primacy, that comes naturally to him, and to us, of constancy and intelligible order? Above all, how can intelligence be conceived as conscious reflection, as an organism that forever bursts outside itself in its very self-manifestation? How are we to think, in Piaget's words, the brokenness and deathliness that invests not only the development of intelligence, but the language and knowledge of the scientist as well? How are we to recall our historical, tenuous, doubtful, living selves, our immediacy in broken forms, our non-necessity, in the order of Piaget's knowledge? The very accuracy of his work, its mathematical and informational correctness, means at once a forgetfulness of how we as knowing beings are in history and in the world.

Does the linear and narrowly empirical nature of Piaget's style and method condemn us to Foucault? Since Piaget, like most of us, is a part of the culture of isolation created in the dominant notions of organism and structure, are we driven to a higher accuracy supposedly residing in

Foucault's style of reflective isolation and doubt?

Foucault's language does have the advantage of reflecting its opposite and giving expression to what is absent in the attention of his vision. He has expressed self-consciously his condemnation, in his manner of description, to the very orders he describes. He has given accounts of the development of the very notions used in the accounts. He has made evident that the issue of his work, on historical self-reflectivity, cannot be given validity by the accuracy of what he says. He has developed an historical science that has broken with an atomistic notion of data and an unfounded, abstract definition of subject matter. He has achieved a measure of clarity in his reflection on the obscurities basic for medicine, linguistics, economics and philosophy.

Where do we look to find order according to Foucault? Not in a world of forms. Not in the mind of God. Not in an instinctual region of the psyche. Not in an isolated text. But in the historical formation of institutions, in the development of language, in the actions of people with each other, in the ways in which opposites and sames reflect each other, in the ways in which separations and kinships develop, in the distances and closeness of things. He appears to have accomplished almost the least predictable of all occurrences: as a French intellectual he seems to have avoided a Cartesian position.

A paragraph from *Madness and Civilization* illustrates the point:

> In the history of madness, two events indicate this change with a singular clarity: 1657, the creation of the *Hôpital Général* and the "great confinement" of the poor; 1794, the liberation of the chained inmates of Bicetre. Between these two unique and symmetrical events, something happens whose ambiguity has left the historians of medicine at a loss: blind repression in an absolutist regime, according to some; but according to others, the gradual discovery by science and philanthropy of madness in its positive truth. As a matter of fact, beneath these reversible meanings, a structure is forming which does not resolve the ambiguity but determines it. It is this structure which accounts for the transition from the medieval and humanist experience of madness to our own experience, which confines insanity within mental illness. In the Middle Ages and until the Renaissance, man's dispute with madness was a dramatic debate in which he confronted the secret powers of the world; the experience of madness was clouded by images of the Fall and the Will of God, of the Beast and the Metamorphosis, and of all the marvelous secrets of Knowledge. In our era, the experience of madness remains silent in the composure of a knowledge which, knowing too much about madness, forgets it. But from one of these experiences to the other, the shift has been made by a world

without images, without positive character, in a kind of silent transparen-
cy which reveals — as mute institution, act without commentary, immediate knowledge — a great motionless structure; this structure is one of
neither drama nor knowledge; it is the point where history is immobilized
in the tragic category which both establishes and impugns it. (p. xii)

I take Piaget and Foucault as both accurate, as I have said. We have
seen that the region of accuracy is not able to account for itself or, taken by
itself, to reflect itself. We have seen the implication that culture founded
in accuracy is founded in self-forgetfulness, that non-accuracy is
fundamental for self-awareness and self-understanding, and that this emphasis on opposition appears to be necessary for us to articulate the
historical awareness fundamental for our intellectual activity.

But how are we to speak of the region where this opposition occurs?
Without a language for the *region* of opposing occurrences, we will be
limited to speaking of finite structures as though they were in common only
by reflecting each other. That appears to be Foucault's position: history is
the region of opposition, and hence of order, in which nothing other than
particular grids of structures are to be found in their historical development. I shall call this position *historical self-reflection.*

The *occurrence* of opposition, however, is unnoticed in Foucault's
historical self-reflection. He has freed himself from all speculative
guarantees of order, such as Hegel's notion of *Geist,* Marx's notion of
historical development, Leibniz' notion of God, and the contemporary notion that reality is fundamentally knowable in either mathematical
systems or self-consistent bodies of facts. After wiping the horizons clean of
non-historical foundations of historical orders, he gives account of the
structures of historically developed orders, and, given his understanding of
order, order seems to be absolute in that order engenders order. Beyond
the accuracy of Foucault's position is an experience of order without an account of the being and disclosiveness of opposition. His position articulates
order and opposition without recall of their eventfulness, and that means
that the structures of order cannot mean their own being.

If structures meant, in addition to the orders they reflect, their own occurrence and if orders meant their own occurrence in addition to their own
historical development, our understanding of both structure and order
would reflect more than their particular historicity. They would reflect as
well how being occurs, how specific visibility is. We shall look at one aspect
of *event* in order to see a direction by which the event of structure and
order may be accounted.

The *non-opposition of opposing situations* and the *nearness of what is distant* are phrases which indicate that opposition is in common as event. The initial observation is that being present or coming forth—being as distinct from not being at all—is a happening that may be described and that *happening* is common for oppositions and differences. Commonality is not only a relation of differentiation. It is as well the event of differentiation in which meaningfulness, concealment, possibility, memory and so forth are in common, even though the specific meanings, hiddennesses and so forth are utterly at odds. Ordering happens in the region of being, and that region is the commonality of historical grids by virtue of their being, and not only by virtue of their similarities and differences in content. In this commonality silence may mean presence of commonality in difference and not primarily irreconcilable difference or a reflection of exclusion.

Concretely, such a recognition on Foucault's part would involve, I believe, an historical account of the space and time of commonality, a region of awareness that does not appear to be available for him. Disorder is found by him to be final within the orders of our time, and exclusion and distance do not seem to be ways in which things happen in common beyond order.

5 Beyond Orders in the Foundation of Intelligence

Piaget's term for ordering principles, *law,* we found, is not reflectively or methodologically based in the historical awareness that he clearly acknowledges. Foucault has founded his interpretation of order in a method of historical self-reflection, but his understanding of order is not founded in the event of distance and closeness with the consequence that opposition and dispersion are thought to control the being of our historical awareness.

A further consequence of Piaget's unfounded notion of law is that for him intelligence tends to be seen as a type of organic development that is not pervaded by the chaos, doubt and creation of the awareness that makes possible forms of discursivity. For Foucault, intelligence, founded in the chaos, doubt and creation of depth and in historical awareness, culminates in a reflective, finite dialectic that is not alert to its own non-dialectical eventfulness.

When the ordered structures of intelligence lack reference either to their own depth of awareness or to their own occurrence, a curious kind of literalism seems always to be present. One may absolutize a method or fix on a set of basic concepts or circumscribe reality with a particular logic. One will tend to identify truth with accuracy according to axiomized rules.

One will tend to be ultimately serious about exactness of reference and formulation. And one will tend to feel, in his/her thinking, the loss of the non-grid, the non-ordered presence of what is. We might note, for example, that *how* things *communicate* their meaning has not played a significant role in our thinking in this discussion. We have not thought out of a sense for communication or *dia-logos* in which meaning happens by virtue of how we come together immediately and communicatively. Intelligence, rather, has tended to be viewed as an organism separate from the reality about which we have understanding. It is also infrequently viewed as founded in a commonality that occurs as presence with each other, as distinct to a private commonality defined by "mental" principles, laws, or structures.

When we interpret ourselves by thinking the commonality of opposites, which is our event, our happening as depth/discursive awareness with all its contrasts, samenesses, spaces, times, relations and disjunctions, we find that structure and order are never sufficient in their totality as a basis for their own understanding. We must also reflect, in our understanding, their event that is their sameness. That means that a complete account of the development of intelligence and a complete account of the depth grids which are the basis for forms of intelligence, if we stop with them, would lead us away from the commonality of our orders and structures, away from the sameness of all that is. When our sameness is not reflected, the pessimism of Foucault is probably right: our language seems to pull away from itself in the very orders to which it gives birth; order means disorder, and disintegration is the likely meaning of all our gathering, hoping, and struggling for commonality without destruction.

References

1 Hans-Georg Gadamer, *Truth and Method* (New York: Seabury, 1975).

2 Jean Piaget, *The Place of the Sciences of Man in the System of Sciences* (New York: Harper & Row, 1970), p. 2.

3 *Ibid.*, p. 3.

Discussion

C. Lee Miller: Could you take your notion of Foucault and Piaget as shadow-images of each other and show us how Foucault would analyze what we heard this afternoon about the child crawling toward the edge of the table? I would like to see what, concretely, Foucault would say we are leaving out if we only take Piaget's analysis of that kind of happening. It makes sense to me when I think of Jung and madness but it doesn't make sense when I think of the child crawling toward the table.

Charles Scott: I would not expect what Foucault says to be relevant to the specific perception of the child who is able to perceive a spatial object and avoid it. I understand that issue in terms of the context of the accuracy itself. The question has to do not with the specific accuracies of Piaget or anyone else. The question has to do with the nature of self-awareness, the kind of self-awareness that is expressed in the very form that an interpretation takes. Most significant would be to interpret the child primarily as a natural organism. The issue has to do with the meaning of nature and natural, and what they mean in the perception of childhood and adulthood. Foucault would characteristically approach the question by what is left out. One would want to find out: what is the shadow of this accuracy and what is the untruth of its validity? That would be the overall context of the methodological self-understanding of the social sciences.

Miller: Is what is left out something that is left out by Piaget or something that the child is leaving out?

Scott: It is something that is left out of the interpretive structure which Piaget articulates . . . or which Foucault articulates. Foucault is persuaded that reality is fundamentally linguistic. Piaget is not persuaded of that. Evolution names a non-linguistic occurrence for Piaget as I understand him. Evolution, for Foucault, names a particular interpretation of events. In that, the notions of progress, linguistic development, and above all, unbroken natural continuity are involved.

Edward S. Casey: I wonder if you are not closer to Piaget than you admit. I certainly do think you have offered a very effective critique of Foucault. But it seems to me that your position concerning opposition is not so radically different from Piaget. At least at one point, you seem to duplicate it in the following sense. It seems to me that Piaget is saying that there is no such thing as a radical conflict in knowledge. For knowledge to exist at all, it must exist within some pre-existent framework composed of a multitude of schemes, some of which may be momentarily out of balance and not in agreement with each other, but which ultimately come into agreement. We do of course have to acknowledge these oppositions at that moment. Perhaps it is the case of the confusing or missing perception. Opposition is built into that very perception itself — but not in the sense of a destructive, conflictual, nugatory, negative sort of thing. On the contrary, it would probably lead to progress in perception itself. Hence the very opposition between two schemes at a given moment in perception is essential. Hence, the shadow, the opposite, the different, the diverse within an organizing order which you call the same or the whole, when translated into Piaget's language, would be something like intelligence or perhaps merely schemes in general. I wonder if there is not a way of putting yourself closer to Piaget than you indicated.

Scott: I certainly am not comfortable going any closer to Piaget than I'm given to. I have enormous admiration for his work. My only hesitancy in affirming what you've asked has to do with the limits of intelligence that I hear in Piaget. *In order to understand intelligence, he wants to do epistemology. In order to understand intelligence, I think one should do ontology.* In order to understand intelligence, he wants to develop a descriptive account of the development of the knowing process. Though accurate, this seems to me nonetheless an inadequate basis to understand the enormous reality called "knowing." Furthermore, the discursive schemes that are fundamentally founded upon discursive continuity is an inadequate basis for understanding perception and relation. As I understand Piaget, this development culminates in a kind of discursivity which is neither enough nor accurate. At every point that I defend Piaget, I feel both immense admiration and the sense that the very reality he is dealing with, namely the nature of knowledge, is distorted by the limits he sets at the outset. That is where I stand right now in relation to Piaget. So yes, I do share probably a sense of continuity more closely with him than with the way I read Foucault. But Piaget's continuity does not tolerate the kind of broken paradoxicality that Foucault has. I think it must before it can understand what "to know" now means.

Casey: This is part of what I would like to hear more about. How radical is the opposition? In one sense, it cannot be so radical as to deny wholeness, since it is itself an aspect of wholeness which I read as an ontological analogue. You certainly say, very radically, that in Piaget's cognitive model, any apparent disharmony will ultimately be brought into some equilibrium—if intelligence is adequate to it. It seems to me that you too are close to that. You do not want to say that opposition is so radical that it cannot ever be reintegrated.

Scott: Well, almost. I would want to say that wholeness does not mean the final integration of oppositions. It means the pervasive commonality of unreconcilable oppositions. If I am wrong in reading Piaget's notion of dialectical contrast to exclude radical brokenness, then he would be closer to Foucault than I portray. Foucault wants to understand opposition by reference to opposition. As a result, he is not able to account for the com-

monality of radical oppositions, a commonality that is necessary for the
comparison he makes. That commonality is not something which, in the
last analysis, would bring them together into a utopian unity. I think he is
right—in the absence of utopia. He cannot speak of the unity that is not a
thing and not harmony. Now Piaget, as I hear him, speaks of a fundamental tendency toward logical harmony or logical relation. That seems to
reflect only one area of contemporary or, let us say, Western human
endeavor. It does not speak of the commonality of fundamental oppositions. So I am not sure about the absence of brokenness in Piaget's account
of mind. I am not sure that there is an analogue, but I very much hope
there is.

Donn Welton: I have a number of questions in this regard. I am having
a lot of trouble trying to sort out the import of your comments. My first impression is that you are really talking about two different levels. One is the
level of ontogenesis, the development of the individual. At that level, you
are conceding that Piaget's description may be accurate. The other level
concerns questions of method. In that respect, you seem to be claiming
that Piaget's naiveté, which you have described in terms of forgetfulness of
historicity and forgetfulness of the world, leads to a kind of false accuracy
based on a distortion in the way he approaches things. I still have difficulty
understanding what that means. Suppose Piaget did not forget the world
or did not make these mistakes. Would that in any way substantially
change his analyses?

Scott: One of the things that I wanted to do for this meeting, but which I
am not yet able to do, is a structuralist account of Piaget's language
regarding accuracy and relation in order to accomplish the sort of thing
you are asking for. If one begins with the observation that human
knowledge is historical or that human intelligence is an historically
developed self-conscious, linguistic event, that is, if one begins with
historical reflexivity in order to understand the perception of objects or the
evolution of the capacity to perceive different kinds of relations, or if one
begins in the context or lived world of the child, then perception would not
be isolated solely to the evolution of a naturalistic or natural genetic
capacity. That would give much greater primacy, as I see it, to what I
would call concrete meanings, but not in Piaget's sense of concrete. It
would give much greater emphasis to the experience and perception of
meanings within which objects stand out as objects to be avoided or
whatever.

Welton: What do you mean by meaning? You mean linguistic immediate meaning, I assume.

Scott: I don't mean that there are meanings other than linguistic or verbal structures. Suppose we begin with the way in which the child builds his world. We would not couch that primarily in quantitative or objective terms. Hence what one discovered in Piaget's work would be a subcategory of a relational kind of investigation. The child begins to experience and recognize, for instance, how opposition occurs, how obstruction occurs, how availability occurs, how transmission occurs, how meaning occurs. The categories to which we have primary reference are the categories of world relation and not primarily the categories of abstract logic. To put it still differently, perception is conceived by primary reference to discursivity and the emergence of meaningful relations. In discursivity and logical structure, Piaget seems to me quite Kantian. I can find no way to reverse your point from him to the lived world without a fundamental shift. I can find a lot from him about the way in which the world may be abstracted, perceived or experienced at a distance.

Welton: Clearly that's not a mistaken notion or an unconscious thing on his part. He has built that into a critique of the Gestaltists. He does so precisely at the point where the Gestaltists, Merleau-Ponty and others sought exactly the kind of thing that you want, namely the emergence of meaning in terms of noematic or ontic structures. Piaget, in a certain sense, is trying to effect almost a Marxist kind of reduction to certain productivities and operations of the subject. Actually, this is one version of Ed Casey's remark. You seem to want to turn a critical eye against Foucault. You tried to introduce the category of event, as a way of establishing the critique, viewing event as somehow the synthesis of structure and history — which you seem to feel is missing in Foucault. Am I correct in that respect?

Scott: What did you say I see event as?

Welton: The synthesis of structure and history.

Scott: The relationship between structure and history, not a synthesis. It is the commonality of oppositions.

Welton: Do you mean by an organism, something which is isolated from its environment?

Scott: I don't mean isolated. I mean distinguishable. Following Piaget, an organism is a self-contained law-abiding entity that generates its own laws. It is law-abiding in the sense that it is the source and development of its own laws. Those laws have to do with how I relate to things. No solipsism is implied. Piaget's description of an organism is basically Kantian, which is not the same thing as either being-in-the-world or the lived world. It is also not the same thing as history, as conceived by Foucault, or tradi-

tion, as conceived by Gadamer. These are three strikingly different alternatives. The contrast means to me that we are still dealing basically with
the history of the knowing subject. This means fundamentally the legacy, a
legacy for which I cannot adequately describe my admiration but which I
want to get away from. I speak primarily of Leibniz and secondarily of
Descartes. I see no way right now to adopt either Piaget's method or his
language — without buying his ontological assumptions. The meaning of
equilibrium is, in part, the primacy of the knowing subject. What he is
describing by *equilibrium* is a continuous process, which relates to the context of meaning and its place within our total scheme of interpretation. In
that larger sense of the scheme of interpretation, equilibrium in Piaget
means a tension of opposites within a knowing organism. Even if we were
to conceive of *equilibrium* in a totally different context, I think the facts
would remain the same. However, we would no longer understand
equilibrium as basically intra-psychic opposition. If we were Foucault, we
would understand it as a fundamental tension within the language. If we
were Gadamer, we would understand it fundamentally as a tension within
the very process of meaning or the self-presentation of meanings. In
another scheme, we would understand equilibrium as not housed in intelligence, but in the way the world occurs, the way language occurs, the
way history occurs, the way tradition occurs. None of these are strictly
mental events. Equilibrium or the concept of space in Hegel would be a
good contrary example to which I suspect I share a resistance with you. But
where do equilibrium and stasis occur in Hegel? Not primarily in a Kan-
tianly conceived mind, intelligence, or reason. It is literally a world event,
which has the meaning of logic. Now contrast the logic of Hegel in its
general direction with the logic of Piaget. In that way, you have a sense of
the difference between stasis, opposition and equilibrium in one and the
other. There is a universe of difference between those two. In Hegel, stasis
and equilibrium are world processes of history. Whatever else Hegel says
historically is probably wrong. What Piaget says about equilibrium is accurate, but in that larger context of the meaning of logic and the meaning
of intelligence, it is from my perspective, forgetful of some things I want to
remember.

Welton: I would disagree with you that structuralism from Piaget's
perspective is not adequate. You suggest a genuine choice between them.

Edward S. Casey: Just a comment on that last question. Isn't it true that
Piaget gets you back into the world and out of the mind because of the concepts of activity or operation? Because of its Kantian origin, "scheme" does
suggest enclosure and mind, and therefore a knowing subject and all the

problems that come with it. But what about the notion of activity or operation? What about the notion that knowledge and intelligence really do
comprehend the situation including the life-world and the world around us
as the potential result of an operation or activity which we might have performed ourselves but in effect we need not have done so in any given case?
To comprehend this lecture hall, for example, would be to comprehend it
as the possible result of an activity which I might myself actually take.
That puts us back into the world again—and a little closer to your
paradigm.

Scott: Would you add to that an understanding of the genetic nature of
operations?

Casey: From the very start, the notion of operation is intimately linked
with the environment or milieu. We are very active in our relation with the
environment.

Scott: That's for sure. That's not in doubt.

Casey: To that extent at least, he does overcome Cartesianism.

Scott: He tends to, but the interaction is of a fundamentally natural,
that is to say, non-worldly entity or organism with a fundamentally world-
ly, non-natural event or reality called world or environment. You still have
got that split in there because the self is not constituted by its history. That
is why Piaget, to be true to himself, does not need to reflect history
methodologically in a Foucaultian way. The very mind it perceives is not
itself intrinsically an historical or natural development. The interaction
will always be modified by a subject/object dichotomy, which is precisely
what has to be overcome in order for us to articulate the historicity of our
own understanding and interpretation.

Casey: Activity seems to me to be something that modifies the environment and actually changes it in such a way as to make it a reflection of our
own intentions and plans. To that extent, we are continuous with it. We
make it what we want it to be within certain actual physical limits and this
is a genuinely dialectical process. "Interaction" was a poorly chosen word
on my part. I think Piaget is more dialectical than that. Piaget does not
present sheer mind confronting some kind of object. Rather, the object is
really reshaped as we transform it.

Scott: Is the agency that shapes and reshapes intrinsically an historical,
linguistic event for Piaget?

Casey: No. That is true. It is not.

Scott: That is my problem right there. I am claiming that to make mind
a self-conscious, intrinsically historical, linguistic event would not fundamentally alter Piaget's "results." It would, however, fundamentally alter

his methodology and his language.

William J. Richardson: You again used the expression: "intrinsically historical, linguistic event." I am asking about language events and the linguistic qualities of events. I take it the phrase "linguistic nature of reality" is in Foucault. I'm wondering if you accept his conception of the linguistic nature of reality. If you do not, then in what way does your own use of the terms "knowledge," "linguistic reality," and "linguistic event" differ from his? If you do, then how do you put that together with your own notion of wholeness as the commonality of irreconcilable opposites?

Scott: I do not accept what I understand to be Foucault's notion of the linguistic nature of reality. I understand him to mean that reality is exclusively a linguistic order when, by *linguistic,* we mean *communicable.* Calling what is linguistic "communicable" is a descriptively accurate thing to say. Institutions, manners, gestures, postures and so forth, are all forms of language. My reasons for rejecting Foucault's circumspection of language, however, is that he understands orders by reference to orders exclusively, and he understands orders to be the genesis of orders. For him, language is a particular and describable history. His way of doing historiography is ontology. The task is to give an account of how things are manifest as opposites, contrasts, antagonists — to show how things are manifest by virtue of being manifest. In the language of the Heideggerian tradition, disclosiveness is describable. The description of manifestness, visibility, or disclosiveness is a description of the commonality of language. It is a description of what is common to all that is manifest and all that is visible, speakable, and referable. That is what I am calling the unity, the same, or the whole. It's not a thing or a substance. It makes no pretentions to eternity or non-eternity. It is the event of reality, disclosiveness, or manifestness. When we get into a position like Foucault's we see that the fundamental structural aspect of all knowledge allows for dissolution and disorder. For him this means that reality itself is fundamentally in question. Its existence is in question. There, I find a kind of realistic, non-prophetic hopelessness. I am deeply disinclined to go for hope for the sake of hope; but I am very much inclined to go for reality or presence for its own sake. I can find none of that in Foucault. In the contemporary setting, language for him is a relation of self-dissolving antagonistic orders or intrinsically self-destructive organisms. Brokenness or perversity would be the fundamental disclosure of the place of our time. For me, that leaves out completely the very occurrence of the reality of perversity or the non-vacuum-like quality of opposition. I am suggesting in this paper that the quality of the being present, of disclosiveness and manifestness is both accessible to description and necessary as a non-order if we are to perceive the meaning of an antagonistic order. If that is true, then opposition is not the fundamental category for understanding the meaning of language. The coming forth of reality is.

FACULTY SEMINAR ON THE CONCEPT OF STRUCTURE IN PIAGET'S GENETIC EPISTEMOLOGY.

Introduction by Donn Welton

Piaget's wager is that the human psyche or the human psychological subject as present in and to the world consists of systems of structures which have not only a synchronic but also a coherent genetic or diachronic relationship to each other. A system for Piaget is not reducible to habits. This is to say that a system is not reducible to the additive effects of conditioning or to however else you would like to define habits. Rather it is much more like a planetary system which, when one of its elements changes, reorganizes itself according to the forces which are inherent in it.

Piaget's attempt to discuss the concept of structure in the text which is before us is both laconic and programmatic.[1] In a certain sense the entirety of his corpus is a progressive definition and exemplification of the notion. Our text is a clearer indication of what Piaget wants to do rather than what he has done with this idea of structure. In these introductory comments, I shall restrict myself to a short explication of the notion of structure and the two examples which exhibit how he attempts to integrate it with the concept of genesis. At the end I will raise a few questions which I hope will stimulate our discussion today.

Perhaps we can define structure as simply as this: structure is a whole or a system of transformations which is self-regulating. Now this is a broad definition. Piaget uses it in many different domains. But I want to try and restrict our considerations, at least initially, to the domain of psychology. Since structure is a whole or a system of transformations which is self-regulating Piaget expressly contrasts a whole to an aggregate.[2] Aggregates are composed of elements which are "independent of the complexes into which they enter,"[3] whereas the elements of a structure, as Piaget suggests, "cannot be singled out or defined independently of the connections involved."[4] Over and against the behaviorists and empiricists, Piaget does not conceive of a whole as a collection of the additive properties of the parts nor does he believe that structure is reducible to the sum of the individual relations holding between the elements. On the other hand he also rejects the Gestaltist thesis that we are at first given wholes in terms of which elements and relations are differentiated. For Piaget it is the *relationship* among elements and then between elements and wholes which is his starting point and this he describes in terms of the principle of generation. "In other words, the logical procedures or natural processes by which the whole is formed are primary, not the whole, which is consequent on the system's laws of composition, or the elements."[5]

The concept of the whole is amplified by Piaget's suggestion that the laws of the composition of a structure are laws of *transformation*. Stability is the result of a regulation brought about by various transformations which continually reestabalish equilibrium (i.e., effect those changes in the structure which restore stasis to the system). Significantly, Piaget defines conservation as the "constant invariant in a system of transformation."[6] Conservation is thus not simply the cessation of motion. It is a kind of invariance within a system which is constantly in tension with itself. Over and against the restriction of the productive elements of constitution to noematic organization, such as you find in the Gestaltists, Piaget considers perceptual objects as well as notions or concepts to be structured by multiple noetic operations, by schemes of transformation. At the same time, schemes of intelligence themselves undergo development motivated by their progressive accommodation to the organization of objects having an instrumental significance. The elaboration of world and intelligence is dialectical and their transformations mutually implicate each other. As Piaget notes, "Every structure has a genesis."[7]

Were psychological structures the result of biological mechanisms or external factors it would be impossible to find a uniquely psychological motivation to mental growth. Recognizing the role of maturation, experience and social transmission, Piaget does not find them sufficient to explain the progression that takes place through stages of development. This progression, he suggests, is rooted in the self-regulatory nature of structure. As Piaget suggests, "The transformations inherent in the structure never lead beyond the system but always engender elements that belong to it and preserve its laws."[8] The principles of development, then, are internal to the system of development. It is their "immanent logic" which carries mental life forward.

In this way I have briefly circumscribed the concept of structure in terms of the notions of equilibrium, self-regulation, transformation and wholeness. I will solidify this view of structure by recourse to a couple of examples. The first example is one which Piaget uses repeatedly to show that perception is irreversible (in the sense of reciprocity).[9] Perceptual estimates, he suggests, always depend upon sequences in which the items are compared. A and B are compared. Then B is compared to C. That is not equivalent to C compared to B; and then B compared to A. If you reverse the sequences, the registrations of length or configuration of lines, for example, are not equivalent. So the Aristotelian formula that A equals A does not hold for perception—precisely because there are other kinds of factors, factors of centration, of environment, context and so forth, which transform the phenomenal presence of the object. In this sense, structures follow an irreversible movement. By simply reversing the direction of the sequence the results are not the same.

According to Piaget there is a step-by-step progression from sensori-motor regulation to operational reversibility. In terms of this progression, we find contributions of intelligence which cannot be reduced to mere modifications of perception. The irreversibility leads eventually to semi-reversibility, because of the activity of sensori-motor and concrete operations; and finally, with the rise of operational intelligence, reversibility is achieved. What accounts for this development is, as Piaget suggests, the coordination of points of view which cannot be understood as the result of perceptual activity *per se*. In Piaget's words, "the forms or structures used by intelligence derive from a genuine construction which has its origins in actions and operations, while perceptual forms are discovered in the object. This discovery, once again, is achieved on the basis of actions, but, in this case, of a very restricted scope, reconstructive, rather than inventive, and never achieving, or even attempting, new constructions."[10] Thus Piaget delineates the fundamental differences between the structure of perception and the structure of intelligence: perception operates in a primarily constructive or reconstructive fashion and focuses on objects in the world, whereas the operations of intelligence arise not so much from variations upon objects as from variations in the subject's activity.

These suggestions are developed in Piaget's example of the child discovering the conservation of a ball of clay throughout its various shapes. Since this example is given in our text, I will only single out one point which helps explain Piaget's suggestion that intellectual structures have their "origins in actions and operations."[11] After noting that there are four phases in the comprehension of compensation Piaget suggests that each stage increases in probability as a function of the immediately preceding stage, not as a function of the point of departure, that is, the simple perception of the ball of clay.[12] The subsequent phases depend upon the development of the scheme of a prior phase or intellectual operation such that the final phase definitely exceeds the reconstructions of perception and introduces fresh contributions which are not reducible to primary perceptual activity.

Having laid this out, we might begin by asking three different kinds of questions. One question would concern the accuracy and validity of Piaget's concept of structure. Especially problematic is the relationship between the concept of structure and the concept of equilibrium. I have just been told, in fact yesterday, that the concept of equilibrium in Piaget has recently undergone a major revision. Perhaps Professor Furth would be able to mention something more about that. In any case, we might ask whether the concept of structure is coherent. Does it make sense? A second kind of question which I would find interesting deals with what psychologists would want to do or what psychologists can do with such a notion. Is there any way in which mainline American psychology (whatever that might be) could find such a concept interesting, suggestive or useful? Lastly, does this notion of structure have applications to other fields? To what extent can this concept be extended in the direction of the natural sciences or in the direction of the interpretation of literature? With these questions I would like to open up the discussion.

Reference

1 Jean Piaget, "Genesis and Structure in the Psychology of Intelligence," in *Six Psychological Studies,* translated by Anita Tenzer. Introduction, Notes and Glossary by David Elkind (New York: Vintage, 1967), pp. 143-159.

2. Jean Piaget, *Structuralism,* trans. by C. Maschler (New York: Harper and Row, 1970).

3 *Ibid.*, p. 7. But contrast *Biology and Knowledge,* trans. by Beatrix Walsh (Chicago: The University of Chicago Press, 1971), p. 139 where even aggregates are taken as a kind of structure but with elementary and external connections such as meeting place and spatial disposition.

4 *Ibid.*

5 Piaget, *Structuralism,* p. 9.

6 Jean Piaget and Bärbel Inhelder, *The Psychology of the Child,* trans. by Helen Weaver (New York: Basic Books, 1969), p. 97.

7 Jean Piaget, *Six Psychological Studies,* p. 149.

8 Piaget, *Structuralism,* p. 14.

9 See Jean Piaget, *The Mechanisms of Perception,* trans. by G. N. Seagrim (New York: Basic Books, 1969), p. 292.

10 *Ibid.*, p. 303.

11 *Ibid.*

12 Piaget, *Six Psychological Studies,* p. 157.

The Faculty Seminar

Roger Schvaneveldt: I will raise a fairly specific question about how Piaget deals with the notion of equilibrium. Let me take it out of the text where he discusses conservation and the problem of why the child is motivated, driven, or whatever terms you want to use, to change from an initial schema that seems to lead the child to pay attention to one dimension of this clay to a situation where the child is taking both dimensions into account. He mentions that one of the factors involved in this transition is subjective dissatisfaction. And I find that sort of troubling in the sense that it seems somewhat *ad hoc* to me. For example, he says that one of the reasons that the child begins to change his mind about whether he should stick with this explanation is that, as a practice of constantly repeating to himself that there is more because it is longer, the child begins to doubt himself. That point seems to come out of nowhere. It has very little relation to the rest of what Piaget is trying to say. I wonder whether someone could enlighten me as to whether this is in fact a central idea for Piaget or whether it is a lapse and someone might provide a stronger motivation for talking about the change in attention from one dimension to more than one. Piaget gives two reasons why, in the second phase, the child begins to reverse judgment and why, in the first phase, the child pays attention to only one dimension. In the second phase, he is likely to reverse and use the other. In the beginning of the second phase, the child reasoning about length would still say it is more but that the stick is longer. This, Piaget says, is the first hint that the child is going to notice this other aspect. Furthermore, there are two reasons which will lead to this change. There's the factor of the central contrast. If you continue to elongate the clay up to the point where it turns into spaghetti then he will end up by telling you, "Oh, no! Now it is less because it is too thin." Some compensation occurs from this other dimension which had previously been ignored until it reaches the extreme state of being so thin that the clay almost disappears. But then he says that the other factor — and this is the one that troubles me — is the notion of subjective dissatisfaction. In effect, I wonder whether the notion of subjective dissatisfaction is really coherent here. Why should the child (after being perfectly successful from the point of view of the child's own schema of accounting for the phenomena before it) now all of a sudden say, "Well, I'm getting tired of saying this?" Is that a reasonable idea? Is it consistent with the rest of Piaget's thought? Is there another formulation that makes it somewhat more intelligible?

Dominic Balestra: May I respond to that? Now this may be the more grand philosophical type of response, but in *Biology and Knowledge* and in the work Piaget did on mathematical psychology and epistemology he gives a constructivist view of mathematics which maintains a certain universality of mathematics and which asserts the emergence of mathematical thought but not a Platonic — that is, pre-given — status. In the end he characterizes a certain perfection on the part of life. By life, he means living forms. He seems to say that in studies of living organisms and embryogenesis there is a fundamental tendency or law on the part of the dynamic organism to extend itself into the environment. Now this is where I agree with you that problems can arise, but I explain the emergence of the cognitive in biogenesis in terms of the organism's programmed need to encompass the environment. Biologically, that program cannot be met. As a result the organism constructs new structures to assimilate its environment. It takes in the entire environment, but in the process, at the cognitive level, the organism has to be transforming the environment itself. Now this might ultimately explain or answer your question. The problem is to talk about it in detail.

Schvaneveldt: I see that as a more promising line actually and not at all the same as the notion of subjective dissatisfaction. Your explanation focuses on the inadequacy of the current schema to take in as much of the environment as possible.

Balestra: Well, I don't think they are incompatible. It may turn out that subjective dissatisfaction has a ring of arbitrariness placing it on the subjective side, and I think that Piaget comes out very much on the subjective side. But not an arbitrary subjective side. There are certain almost law-like characteristics that govern the development of the subject and how the subject structures his world. That's not arbitrary. But it is subjective. However, I don't know whether that subjective dissatisfaction also has an affective component.

Schvaneveldt: In part, I am responding to that and in part to just the bare notion itself. Piaget wants to say that subjective dissatisfaction arises as a function of repetition — sheer repetition. It's something analogous to boredom, I suppose. One gets tired of saying the same thing about the same situation all the time.

Edward S. Casey: I wonder if it's really a matter of an actual feeling state. It seems to me that Piaget talks mostly about cognitive dissatisfaction in such a way as not to imply that the child is actually experiencing dissatisfaction as such. It seems to be just Piaget's way of trying to comprehend this process. For the child as such, it may not be experienced as dissatisfaction. It may be repetition which, suddenly on the eleventh step, leads to difference. Inference would have to be interpreted here as dissatisfaction with firsthand repetition, but I'm not sure he would want to say that it actually reaches a state of what we would call the sense of dissatisfaction. Hence, as I take it, the phrase is misleading.

Susan Buck-Morss: I think it's very leading. Rather than go the route of trying to make Piaget more coherent by this biological metaphor which I find very suspect anyway, I prefer to try extricating him from this problem. That very weak point that you put your finger on can lead us to a real lacuna which demonstrates the rim of his vision in such a theoretical position and the necessity of making his thesis continuous. Such a reorientation would probably lead in the direction of Freud. In reference to that kind of subjectivity I once tried to look at the Freudian development model and the Piagetian development model. My African trip, however, led to an entirely different article. Yet it seems to me that the two theories cannot be put side by side, that their axes fall in different places and have a different kind of relationship to each other. I'd love to hear what you would have to say about that.

Casey: Well. I'm just thinking that what I mean is what Freud would say. Freud would probably posit feelings of dissatisfaction and make them into specific motives for cognitive change. But Piaget doesn't commit himself to the thesis of affective states as necessarily present or as motives for change.

Buck-Morss: That is much more complex than the biological notion, and the analogy is much simpler and more esthetically pleasing. I think it suits Piaget better.

Balestra: It's not really an analogy. In *Biology and Knowledge*, his whole point is to make that analogy . . .

Buck-Morss: He wants to say it is not merely an analogy, but I'm afraid he's wrong.

Sandy Petrey: Isn't it saying in effect that this is an experiential introduction of a subsequent conceptual study and that this subjective dissatisfaction leads to the recognition of two dimensions which do not happen as the result of experience but only as the result of intellectual maturation?

Buck-Morss: That's right.

Donn Welton: Oh, no! If you mean by maturation, something that is tripped off in the organism stage by stage, it is obviously not that. Even on this point I think that the discussion has gone way afield in a certain sense because the answer may be rather simple. If you tried to reconstruct this theoretically, it might be something like this: the child is operating with clay and as long as he still operates with it within certain parameters there is no problem—he'll never move on to the next stage. However, once he stretches it out to a certain level, he realizes that there's a kind of inconsistency in the types of operations that he's been doing . . . in relation to the schemes that he now has—intellectually. In that kind of a bind one could look for some sort of motivation between the two. In other words, the activity itself outstrips the interpretive schemes which are available to the child.

Schvaneveldt: Then I don't understand why he doesn't stop with factor one. That is essentially what factor one says: you keep making the clay thin enough and all of a sudden its thinness begins to overwhelm its length. And that does create a problem. So why go on to the next step of talking about subjective dissatisfaction? That was my question.

Welton: You're asking whether there are two motivations involved: (1) something analogous to what I was talking about; and (2) something else called an "urge" or "desire" or "subjective dissatisfaction."

Schvaneveldt: I agree in a sense. Factor one doesn't seem to be quite enough by itself. The scheme that the child has of focusing upon this one dimension is perfectly adequate to the task. One could do that forever and still cope with the situation at hand. What we need to explain is why the child goes beyond that. It is one of the problems I find in Piaget's theory—the problem of equilibrium that you [Donn Welton] mentioned in your question: it is hard to find the source of change. While all of the elements seem to be there—the question of why the development takes place is not clear—that gap isn't quite closed.

William J. Richardson: Donn, you rejected the word "maturation." If you reject that, what sense do you make out of a phrase which you use yourself, namely an "immanent logic of the developmental process?"

Welton: It would be a function of an interaction in the absence of which we would not have the development. The term "maturation" connotes the idea that certain subjective or internal mechanisms would be tripped off automatically, regardless of the development of that relation.

Schvaneveldt: But then how do you account for that?

Balestra: But Piaget says you get three factors: (1) maturation or internal, hereditary factors; (2) the influence of the physical environment; and (3) the experience or exercise of various social transmissions. He has all three of them going.

Welton: His point is that you can read them into a given situation, though they in themselves are not sufficient conditions. I am not saying that maturation or social factors do not exist. But you are looking for an instinctively psychological logic to development. It seems to me that the notion of maturation inadequately accounts for what he wants.

Hugh J. Silverman: William Richardson's question focuses on the status of a human logic. Consider an alternative model—which is just a model—for example Thomas Kuhn's account of the development, or history, of science. For Kuhn, the movement from one conceptual scheme as a way of "doing" science to a new one indicates a sudden paradigm shift from one type of scientific understanding into a new one. It seems that Piaget is giving a very similar account in terms of the child's understanding. Take his example of the clay. Consider that there are three stages here (not stages in Piaget's sense but three moments). In one moment, a piece of clay is in the shape of a ball, while the other is elongated and looks (to the child) greater in quantity than the first piece. The second moment is an intermediary stage in which the child notices some discrepancy but is unsure what it means. At a final stage, the clay is extended so much that it shifts over into a new conceptualization for the child. Naturally the child must be at the threshold of a shift to begin with. The point is that there is an internal logic to the child's reconceptualization. Hans Furth characterized an "immanent logic" yesterday when he said that the mind was in the object. So subjective dissatisfaction is not so much *my* dissatisfaction or the *child's* dissatisfaction as opposed to some external relations within the object itself. Rather this dissatisfaction—call it "subjective"—is already in the cognitive formulation of the object as such.

Charles Scott: The way I verbalize this is basically in agreement with what Hugh said and I want to see if you would object to this. Subjective dissatisfaction in Piaget's terms is a conflict of structures that are immediate in their own development and a conflict that occurs in the relationship of the assimilative and accommodative functions. So the term "subjective dissatisfaction" names an impersonal or a non-personal clash that occurs in the cognitive, perceptive experience. Maybe that implies a certain notion of subjectivity. I'm not sure that it does. But it would not be used to indicate the emergence of another reality—namely a judging, experiencing subject. Rather it would name the immediate experience, or I think Bill Richardson's term was the immanent experience of structures constitutive of the knowing organism. These structures are, in a certain sense, dissociative. The organism itself is modified by a non-coherence in the specific function of assimilation and the specific function of accommodation.

Casey: You have identified the notion of "subject" which Piaget develops in his book on structuralism — that is, the subject which is dissatisfied. It is not the personal subject. It is not the feeling subject. It is the epistemic subject — the subject which is common to all subjects in that situation and whose structure would be identical throughout. The dissatisfaction would be some kind of generalized or universal dissatisfaction. If it means anything at all, it would have to be the kind of dissatisfaction that everyone in that situation and with that clash would feel.

H.J. Silverman: It is the subject which is involved in the self-regulating. It is the self of self-regulation.

Casey: This other form of subject is what we are discussing and it is certainly problematic itself. That is not an answer either but at least it indicates the direction in which an answer could perhaps be found.

Hans Furth: Piaget is very dissatisfied with what he has written. He has written another book on equilibrium where he starts off saying that this former model is quite unsatisfactory. So I find myself in a difficult situation, and I don't know what Piaget would say to this. Piaget starts off by indicating five insufficiencies to that model which we have in front of us. The main point is that for him this model is too subjective. When something happens inside it is just "subjective dissatisfaction." Piaget has tried to include the object in this new model. As you know he will say that, for the child, the object changes in terms of what the child sees out there. It is not just what the child feels. Nor is it schemes. The object is something different for the child. There is no place for the subject/object distinction. The difference is between what the child registers as observable and what the child interprets as coordination. This changes. The other point is related to the nature of contradictions. Contradiction is built into knowing. All knowing deals with contradictions and compensations. Piaget would say that what a child considers both the length and width is not a contradiction. The child does not even see it as a contradiction. The child simply says that it is more. It does not occur to the child that there is any contradiction. When the child begins to experience some contradiction, then it turns out that the contradiction is nothing other than that which confirms the child's scheme. What is experienced as contradiction becomes confirmation of a different viewpoint. He deals a lot with the place of contradictions and compensations, and the point that all knowledge carries within it the seed of contradiction and compensation. Knowledge is nothing else but a balance of compensations that will by themselves lead eventually to new contradictions. So I tried to indicate yesterday how Piaget sees it in terms of the observable and the subjective. Piaget would be the first person to say that he is not satisfied with simply talking of probability and subjective insufficiency. I do not even believe that experiential explanation shows that children are dissatisfied. They are not upset if I can't solve this problem. I mean, they are not unhappy about it at all.

L. Theresa Silverman: It seems to me that there are certain stages when the child experiences frustration.

Buck-Morss: But that's a different thing though. That's not an epistemic subject which experiences frustration but the whole child. And I don't think that you can block out the affective psychology of the child in that experience. Isn't it possible to interview the child going out feeling a little bit queasy about what was going on?

Furth: I interview children on the understanding of business and money. Five or six year old children think that you pay money, the shopkeeper gives you money back and it's just like a ritual since you shake hands. Then some children begin to understand that you have to pay for things. You then ask them if the storekeeper has to pay for things. I remember one child who says, "I think I understand that. It's like me going to the shop . . . the storekeeper has to go to another store." You could say that I have experienced that the child has had an insight. But the child wasn't frustrated before. He was excited that he understood in the sense that he enjoyed talking about it. I can experience this. But really frustration, if it comes to dissatisfaction, is a rather sophisticated experiential thing that you won't find among children.

Unidentified: The example we have been belaboring does not give us enough data. If the report stops at the point where the child finally says whatever the experimenter has in mind, more could be involved. Have we really seen a glimpse of the next stage in some conservation notion or do we simply have one answer to a question which has been asked ten times in a row? Finally, the child gives you a different answer. But is it dissatisfaction with a situation or dissatisfaction with the discrepancy between schema and perception?

Balestra: It's something like when I say the right thing, he will let me out of here.

Josef Nivnik: Having read this chapter and another book on structuralism, I'd like you to go back to the first question concerning the notion of structure. It seems to me that we may have expected too much from Piaget in regard to this question. I think that discussion has shown that child psychologists do not use the word structure. Piaget in general is quite careless about the word. In defining structure, he gives only three points for understanding what he means by structure. Later, however, he does not use it in a precise way. For example, with reference to "love of brother" he is quite careless about putting together love and brother. It is not clear what kind of love he means here, but it is certainly not any precise meaning. He is also quite careless about the word "structure." In fact this is just a substitute for such phrases as "stage of development in child psychology" or "psychology of intelligence" or "stages of efforts" or something of the sort. In general, he does not need this word. For other purposes it is just economy, word economy. Expecting something from the word "structure" is justified when taken in the direction of structuralism or Lévi-Strauss' structural anthropology which is based on exact rules, or exact methods and exact word use. Then we can follow certain prescribed states in dealing with material in which the word "structure" is useful. When it serves only as a substitute for several other words, it may be very useful but we shouldn't expect any methodological rigor from it. Furthermore, I myself would not expect such rigor.

Welton: This may be a function of the essay that we chose as much as anything else. We were limited in what we could do. There are other cases which are much more detailed and give the kind of law that you're looking for. Such books as *Mechanisms of Perception* offer a highly detailed discussion of exactly what you want. If it is just a question of whether or not the term is being used in a loose way, the problem may be that we are discussing a ten-page essay. What I would want to know in this connection is whether or not there is something about the way in which he has defined structure in terms of these notions of self-regulating system, systems of transformation and wholeness which is not equivalent to the laws regulating the relationships between the individual parts.

Dick Howard: I think that there might be. In this regard, Saussure begins with the arbitrariness of the sign and its social nature. What strikes me in Piaget is the isolating of the individual. First, learning is a social process. If I watch my own kid, or if I watch other kids, or if I talk to students in a lecture hall, it is not an individual learning process but a group learning process. Actual learning behavior among children would be group behavior and not something isolated in terms of the individual. Second, learning behavior is working behavior. For example, in regard to the clay, the experimenter is doing things to the clay. I wonder what would happen if the child were doing these elongations with the clay. Would this set up a different situation? Because of those two problems — if I am right that they are crucial notions and that they are not taken up by Piaget — it would seem that his appropriation of structuralism, its implications as a scientific method and its linguistics as the first social science is built on a science of the individual. The implication is that his use of structure is seemingly quite careless. I may be wrong about whether Piaget does isolate the individual in that way. And I may be wrong about my two assumptions about learning.

Balestra: May I say something in favor and partly in response to what you said? I'm not familiar at all with Saussure and the other structuralists. In fact, I came to Piaget from the philosophy of science. I've done a lot of work in the history of science and mathematics. Twentieth century mathematics is structural. In effect, it is pure structuralism. The object for mathematics in the twentieth century is a structure. The Bourbaki have done a tremendous job in making the point evident. This is what attracted me to Piaget. Look at physics today. Physics is wedded through and through with mathematics. To that extent, the ontological status of theoretical instances is made evident. Physicists are now studying structures — mathematical structures. If structuralism is that precise in mathematics, it will surely lose its precision as you move into the physical domain, but it may still not cease to be a good tool. For me, it helps to get a handle on the post-Kuhnian problems in the philosophy of science. Right now the Darwinian populational model poses a number of problems because it remains too much at the level of analogy with a lot of quick comparisons. Piaget may be very resourceful there. If we have learned anything today from the philosophy of science it is from work in meaning theory. Scientific theory is a structural entity. Independent parts from wholes. Meanings among the concepts of science in the history of science are subject to transformations. In this respect, the Piagetian approach has much to offer. It would be nice if it could lead to a grand synthetic instrument that could relate all the sciences — but I don't know how resourceful that would be. In mathematics it works beautifully.

Buck-Morss: What do you mean: "in mathematics it works beautifully?"

Balestra: What I mean is that if you delineate the history of mathematics using Piaget's notion of structure and then use functional mechanisms to explain the growth of knowledge, it works out beautifully.

Buck-Morss: Because he says that the ontogenetic and the phylogenetic developments are not the same?

Balestra: They apparently don't look like they're the same. It looks like the beginning of Euclidean geometry. This is the apparent discrepancy. In the child what comes first are topological structures. In Euclidean geometry, there is the emergence of very sophisticated, determined and precise structures. In mathematics, fundamental structures such as the topological, algebraic and order structures may begin contemporaneously. What we really need in order to have a phylogenetic history is to have a special man back there watching man before he became too sophisticated. In other words, human beings existed hundreds of years before Euclid. I would like to have been there to see what kind of mathematical concepts were operative then. That doesn't refute Piaget. It simply does not confirm him either. Do you see my point about the phylogenetic appeal? In evolutionary theory there is a parallel ontogenesis and phylogenesis. It has to be used cautiously but it can also have heuristic value. So I don't think that the objection holds.

Casey: What you say reminds me that in this article one of the major whipping posts is Husserlian phenomenology which seeks to examine any philosophy or science that claims to have an absolute beginning. When discussing mathematics, Husserl characteristically focuses upon geometry as in his essay called the "Origin of Geometry." He seemed to regard geometry as the most important transmissible form of mathematical knowledge — or at least that form which phenomenology could explicate. Husserl characteristically picks up the most adult — the last stage of development — as what he would normally call noematic, or purely formal, content. Phenomenologists and perhaps philosophers in general, like Plato with his over-dramatization of geometry, seem to overlook the whole of what we would call the symbolic and the pre-operational. Their conceptualizations really do not fit and cannot cope adequately with what you were calling earlier stages of development and so on.

Balestra: Today with Gödel's results there is not only no absolute beginning but also no absolute end. Hilbert's formalistic program was based on a similar hope. It is now falling apart. That meshes very well with Piaget's theory of genesis as having an apparently temporal formal structure. What I find fascinating is how you get something atemporal out of genesis which is itself temporal. I'm not sure you can pull it off, but it looks like Piaget is doing a good job of it.

H.J. Silverman: I wonder if we could come back to a point that Dick Howard made about the particularly social function of structures and the productive work which is involved. What about the ego-centric aspect which Piaget describes in terms of the earlier stages of the child's development? In principle, the child integrates whatever the other does into his own conceptual perspective. Perhaps Hans Furth could say something about that — at least in response to the particularly social concern. Is not egocentrism nevertheless a social phenomenon — for example, by negation?

Furth: The child's development of the self is correlative with the child's development of understanding others — and understanding society. There is no split where the child first understands himself or herself and then projects the thing to others. It is simply contemporaneous. So the idea of a child developing apart from society is just contradictory. There's nothing in Piaget that would even suggest this. Of course, Piaget hasn't worked it out. Others must follow through as I and others are doing now at Catholic University. The word "egocentric" is one of the terms which Piaget says he wishes he had never used because it is so easily misunderstood. Probably all it means is that the child — even at the sensori-motor stage — fails to distinguish between self, action and object. There is a progressive decentration which is part of the intellectual development. The child of preschool age is still primarily unable to do this decentration. That is what Piaget means by egocentric. It does not mean selfish or preoccupied with self. It simply means that the child thinks from his or her viewpoint, and this viewpoint is quite personal.

H.J. Silverman: But cognitively this is not an asociality?

Furth: Not at all. That is precisely where this word is completely misunderstood. If anything Piaget has always stressed that the child learns much more from his or her peers than from adults. It is obvious that the child is much more interested in what other children are doing than in what adults are doing.

Howard: But then how does that work into the theoretical model, for example as you discussed it yesterday?

Furth: Well, Piaget does not describe actual situations. Piaget describes the schemes that are in the child. Within this viewpoint, my scheme is my scheme — it is not your scheme. Piaget describes my personal scheme as part of the development of the person.

Howard: In the model which you presented yesterday, what about the observed object?

Furth: The event can be another person. The event can be interpersonal relations. The event is open . . . it could be anything.

Howard: But things could be very different. For example, the child crawling across the floor toward the table and the child crawling toward his mother.

Furth: From a certain viewpoint they would be different. But from another viewpoint they could be very similar. If you have an interest in spatial knowledge, it makes no difference whether the child is crawling toward the table or crawling toward his mother. The mother is in the way just as the table is also in the way. It depends upon what you are interested in. The model is open-ended.

Buck-Morss: Is the knowing subject separable from the whole subject? You said that you thought it was a problem. Do you see a direction that you have to go in order to reach a solution to that problem?

Casey: That's related to Dick Howard's question.

Furth: That's right. That's exactly what it is. Piaget is interested in the knowing subject, and he is interested in the child insofar as the child is a knowing subject.

Buck-Morss: The question is whether in Piaget it makes any difference whether the object is a mother or a table. Absolutely true. For the epistemic subject, it would not make a difference. Is the epistemic subject simply a myth that Piaget invents and uses simply because it works?

Furth: All scientists invent their own perspective and then forget everything else. There is no other way of using our intelligence.

Casey: The epistemic subject is comparable to Kant's notion of the transcendental subject. It is the transcendental subject now brought to developmental psychology. It makes perfect sense. It is necessary and must be posited. Part of the job of philosophy is to see to what extent the notion is adequate to the actual situation. Does Piaget's theory correspond to a coherent subject? The notion of a positive subject or substratum is necessary in order to bring together all these otherwise diverse and completely variegated schemes. It would be a kind of container or repository for schemes that we would call the epistemic subject. Does this in fact have experiential components? Does it correspond at all to our own sense of adult self and so on? Well, I don't know. These are the questions we would have to go on to ask. At least Piaget's preliminary positing of it is perfectly valid. It may even be necessary. But I'm not at all sure that even if we said: "Well, this seems perfectly arbitrary and only a function of your system," and even if one has to stick to it once one adopts it, I'm not sure that would upset Piaget. I think he would say: "Well sure, that's just part of my procedure as a scientist." He would not worry about its non-experiential or even its anti-experiential components. In a way here is a point where dialogue between philosophers or at least phenomenologists and Piaget becomes very difficult. Maybe not all philosophers would find this as problematical as I was suggesting. Because Kantians would have a much easier time accepting this, they would welcome it and embrace it.

Scott: Let me ask an elaborative question in that regard. For Kant, as I understand him, the structures of knowing are experiential structures.

Casey: Structures of experience!

Scott: That's right. They are structures of experience. And they are only found in experience — methodologically. Now that seems very close to what I understand Piaget to be doing. I understand the process of assimilating to be very close to what Kant means by experience. And associating for Piaget is very close to what Kant means by thinking. But in any event I am really addressing Ed Casey at this juncture in terms of this distinction between knowing and experiencing that you give in quasi-Kantian terms. I understand you to be saying that a phenomenological perspective of experience is designed to deteriorate the Kantian notion of experience or to broaden it out and reconstitute it. From another viewpoint Piaget is dealing precisely with structures of experience. In the name of what do we isolate this region of experience called "the epistemological" or the "knowing" from the actual occurrence of experience or experiencing that is so much larger? For methodological reasons we need to be clean and restricted. But is it in the name of abstract clarity that we do that? We thereby simply say that what we know about the knowing subject is distorted from the beginning by virtue of the arbitrariness of the limits? Or is there a justification for saying that this experience is to be our region of clarity in order to understand the education and the development of the child? How do you understand this limit on experience from a transcendental viewpoint?

Casey: Your sense of "transcendental" here seems much richer than Kant's. You are positing a very deep ontological base called "occurrence" from out of which we have both what we would call personal experience or "experiencing" as Dewey called it and then a higher level comprising the structures of that experience — structures which make that experience possible. That's what Kant was concerned about. In fact, you seem to be proposing three levels of analysis. The third is some sort of primordial ground, which is non-specified historically or developmentally. It is what I think you're getting at when you say that we don't need to be neat at that level because neatness is not an issue.

Scott: I just mean simply that there is a table that the child goes around and that there is a mother that the child goes around. To ignore that is obviously to ignore a real part of the experience.

Schvaneveldt: I don't see why the difference is ignored necessarily. It really is an oversimplification to say that even in Piaget's theory the schema for dealing with mother is of the same sort as the schema for dealing with table. One schema clearly has to be much more complex than the other.

L. T. Silverman: I think that you can look at the child.

Buck-Morss: She's speaking as a mother . . .

L. T. Silverman: No, as a table. You can look at what the child is doing, and if the child is focusing on some sort of spatial orientation, whether tables, mothers, cats or whatever, the movement or the concentration of the child is the same. If, on the other hand, the child's activity is directed toward social phenomena, obviously at that point in time, the mother is differentiated from the table. But they are two different types of cognitive acts, and you can tell from what the child is doing which the child is experiencing.

Buck-Morss: It may be very different when the child can think of only one thing at a time. When I want to walk through space, I can't also think of you as mother except perhaps at times. Maybe something very different is going on in the child than in the adult who brackets out everything except that one thing he or she is capable of.

Scott: Well, deal with possibility for example. Let's say that the child is in the process of going around the table and is injured or hurt. And he is going around the mother and he is hurt. The child in his hurt or in his need will respond, I believe, quite differently to the table than to the mother. Now I would say that is an indication that the child's response depends in some way or to some extent upon the mother. I would say that is an indication of intrinsic possibility, which constitutes the experience and the capacity to respond differently in the experience. If that capacity to respond differently to the table than to the mother is constitutive of experience, then it seems that a fundamentally different kind of experience is indicated. To say that it is only a matter of spatial relation is to abstract tremendously from the constitution of the event in which the child may reach out or turn away as an intuitive response to pain in this situation. In other words, an experience has to be defined, in part, by reference to what can and cannot occur in other conditions of the same situation.

Balestra: But doesn't Piaget's theory itself have a means of incorporating that distinction. If you talk about scheme as formed by interaction with the world, then the interaction that one has with mother is much more elaborate than the interaction that one has with table. Spelling that out alone is going to account for a great difference.

Furth: The experience of table for the child is not separated from the experience of the place where the table is or where the mother is or where the home is. Piaget never dreamed that a child developed a concept of table apart from the concept of mother. And every child develops his or her world within a context in which he or she lives. And that includes the mother, for example. Piaget doesn't study the concept of pain. If he did, he would of course discriminate the child's relation to the table from his relation to his mother. But if you study the concept of space, then you are dealing with a different question.

Scott: It's not clear to me that the space of avoiding table is identical at all with the space of avoiding mother. The assumption seems to be that space is a structure, a reality that is abstractly independent of its situation. It is not yet clear to me that space is one thing like a form of substance. This is what I hear in Piaget. In other words, it seems to me that the study of the perception of space is not properly separated from the event of space.

Furth: For Piaget, space is the activity of the child. The mother is the activity of the child. Basically, the two situations are similar. Most of the child's activity in space involves dealing with other persons. Space is an abstract thing only for us eggheads. For the child, space means moving around, going to mother, going there, wanting something, showing off in front of somebody. If Piaget excluded the social aspect he could be faulted. He doesn't exclude the social. You could just as well write that he excludes the physical. For Piaget, space means the child's activity. The child's activity is primarily a social activity. He didn't say that it is activity toward social objects or physical objects. It's activity. The difference between personal and physical is developed much later anyhow. If the child is hurt by the table, the child is going to talk to the table as if he were talking to a person. "Why did you hurt me?" We make the distinction. A child doesn't make the distinction.

Casey: Well. Right. But a problem remains. We are not children anymore; we are here trying to make sense of Piaget's theory of the child in relation to the table or in relation to the mother. Piaget does have a specific set of schemes for mothers and for close parental figures (he calls them affective schemes) in which he at least in part and even specifically takes account of the way in which persons, and especially important persons, feature in the child's development. What I don't find is how those affective schemes relate to the purely spatial scheme. Is there any way in which these two are brought together in Piaget?

Furth: He has affective schemes for a security blanket. In the final analysis, Piaget would way that he is not a psychologist. Piaget studied space as we adults and scientists decided to name space. He is interested in how the child got from where he or she was born to this knowledge. Piaget did study the self-structure. Affective schemes is just a general term to describe how the child is affected by certain persons or things.

Casey: There is one passage in *Memory and Intelligence* where he seems to say that the most crucial affective schemes concern the primary figures, namely, the parents. He recognizes the need for more affective critical schemes which help us understand a little better why the mother differs from the leg of the table. But we still don't know how the scheme of mother, if there is such a thing, is related to an indifferent scheme such as that of a table leg.

Furth: I would like to offer one, or perhaps the, most crucial difficulty that I see in Piaget. For Piaget, structure and development are synonymous. The cognitive structure is that which develops. For Piaget, there is a structural or cognitive component in any behavior. Now the crucial problem is that what Piaget seems to mean when he talks of development is cognitive development and everything else is a consequence of cognitive development. When we talk about emotional development for Piaget, we really mean cognitive development applied to emotions. And when Piaget studies cognitive development, he really thinks he is studying the development of the child. Whatever the type of development whether it be musical, affective, social or societal, the development component is the cognitive component. And that is what Piaget studies. When Piaget talks about affective schemes he is just paying lip service. He has not really studied it. He just says: "Sure enough, I know they are there."

Balestra: Would it be accurate to say then that, for Piaget, there can be no personal subject without a cognitive subject?

Furth: Of course not.

Balestra: This is where I had a little tension. I don't think he has a transcendental subject, while he does have a cognitive subject. But that seems to be universal.

Furth: That's the epistemic subject.

Balestra: When he talks about me as a knowing self, he robs me of everything that makes me me. He talks about only that which is universal. How do you reintroduce the concrete me? That's what I see as a tension.

Furth: It is related to what I said before. The cognitive component is the basis of what makes you human. That is why we can talk to each other. That is why we are both human. Is the cognitive component the only human component? In some ways it is a very difficult question. Can we talk about social and affective development separately?

Schvaneveldt: Using your argument of a moment ago, does the child make the distinction between the cognitive, the affective and the epistemological? The idea that the child distinguishes between the affective schema, which is appropriate for certain other things, and a positive schema is really quite foreign to Piaget's way of thinking.

Casey: That was the point. These are instruments of knowledge and not objects of knowledge. For the child, they are not objects. That's clear. Nevertheless Piaget is positing them as they are operative in the child. So we have to take them seriously and we have to take the distinction seriously. We have to worry about how they're related to each other even if the child does not. So it is no less of a problem.

Schvaneveldt: Also it is we who are deciding that whatever is being posited is free of affective components. I prefer to give Piaget the benefit of the doubt here and to say simply that he has not studied that question. At least it is not the focus of his study. Someone else might do it differently and prefer to study that component. But Piaget has made a choice.

Scott: That's a huge choice.

Schvaneveldt: I agree.

Furth: When Piaget studies images and symbols he leaves out the affective, although he does mention it in his book on symbols. Nevertheless he is still interested in the cognitive epistemic component. That is why, in many ways, all his books are misnomers. He is constantly focusing upon this one epistemic question.

Schvaneveldt: Does Piaget explain why a child will choose to behave according to one of many schemata?

Furth: Do you mean why he goes over to the table or to the chair?

Scott: If space is constituted by relations of meaning, which are not identical with the activities of a cognitive individual, but are structures in which cognitivity and affectivity arise, then to understand space as an activity of an individual is either an uninteresting kind of reality or a loss of the reality of space itself. Space, in this case, would be something that I'm in as a function of close and near, threatening and attractive, and so forth. Those would be the structures of space. I respond to them.

Furth: You are correct in saying that Piaget did not study space. Piaget studied the scientific concept of space and how that develops in the child. For that purpose, Piaget thought he could leave out the subjective experience of personal space. We talk about development. A person who is overpowered by his personal experience won't ever be able to understand scientific space.

Claude Evans: Isn't that precisely the methodological problem which you run into here? You say you are starting with the scientist's concept of space, thinking of how that develops in the child. You are assuming that that does develop in the child. Yet it seems to me that you may be doing something else. The scientist is using his concept of space when looking at what the child is doing. The scientist is not looking at the concept that the child is developing. The child's space may in fact be very different. Two different things are at work here.

Balestra: But the child learns physical space. Maybe that's a better term. The child does not study the space that Einstein or Hilbert examined. But children do study the way physical objects are related. When driving a car you need some kind of working knowledge of space.

Furth: Then this arises out of a particular person. Piaget says how this develops in general.

Schvaneveldt: There is an interesting difference here. Adults that drive cars may not drive cars according to the scientist's conception of space.

Buck-Morss: As a matter of fact, you have to be able to become almost impervious to space to drive a car correctly.

H.J. Silverman: It seems to me that Piaget incorporates spatiality into what you call the scientist's conception of space. Driving a car involves both a sense of space and the actual geometrical relations. Studying the child in the sensori-motor stage involves both the sense of space and particular distances. Both are included in the same concept.

Casey: And another side of this is a much more Heideggerian notion which I think Charles Scott is getting at. This side is really not subjective at all, but in fact on the contrary it is highly objective, or at least impersonal. It is precisely that from out of which the abstract, the personal, the subjective and even physical space are differentiated in a Heideggerian conception.

Scott: Or Merleau-Pontian perspective.

Casey: Or what we could call a phenomenological conception of space. At least, this has to be taken seriously. Maybe there is some other more general or generalized sort of space.

Balestra: Topological space. We were talking about subjective distances. Topology is the study of regions — connectedness and disconnectedness. Topology abstracts from distance functions, measuring and Euclidean parallel lines.

H.J. Silverman: You don't want to claim that Piaget's notion of space is topological space do you?

Balestra: No. But that is surely part of it. When Piaget was rather young he wrote a critique of Kantian categories showing that they are not *a priori*. And what does he study? He studies Kant's space . . . Kant's time . . . substance . . . Kant's category of causality . . . those categories which are necessary to natural science. He set out to show that they do truly evolve. Everyone had their children around — Locke and Descartes — but no one bothered to consult them. If they had, they would have found that "Gee, you know it doesn't work." Piaget is quite right when he says that the two-month old baby doesn't have a conception of the permanent object or objects of substances in that kind of Kantian way.

Welton: In listening to the discussion, the key question seems to be a methodological one. Are we generating a certain stand-off between Piaget's empirical methods, which are necessarily going to involve him in certain kinds of abstractions, and what Professors Casey and Scott are looking for; that is, something more like a phenomenological kind of approach. I'm wondering whether or not you have an either/or option. If you do a phenomenological description of certain ready-to-hand structures or more subjective ways of dealing with space (as Merleau-Ponty and Sartre have done), does that mean that Piaget's work is of the empiricist, scientific sort? Then you have to worry about Piaget's retort that there is no way of confirming and disconfirming these matters with well-established theories. My question is whether there is any way of putting those kinds of perspectives together.

Casey: It was suggested that there is a solution. Topology, as an early form in the growth of the child's conception of space, does correspond to a Heideggerian conception. At least it seems to in terms of the descriptive notions of closeness, nearness, regions and so on. This is the formal analog or model of what Heidegger describes as primordial, indeed, more primordial than any ontological model of it. The division is still present. It seems that there is no way of overcoming it through formal models *per se*, for they are the schematic aspects of space. Real development is absolutely intrinsic and not to be denied. That doesn't mean that the schematic aspects exhaust the ontological features of such development.

Furth: Can I ask you what you mean by primordial? Do you mean how it appears to the infant?

Casey: No. No. Nothing of it appears to the infant at all.

Furth: Well, that is the whole thing. The very notion of saying that there is space is our way of talking about it. The infant doesn't differentiate between self, space and actions, which are all adult categories. What then do you mean by primordial?

Casey: I mean that which adults and particularly Heideggerians live. This primordial space is also the child's space — especially the first space of the child. But we adults also have our rights. We have the right to posit primordial space too. I don't think that there is any reason to believe that because we come to experience space first in such and such a way as children that that space is more basic than our present space or the space that we wish to posit.

Furth: But is there agreement among adults about what is primordial?

Casey: No there is not. There is no way of resolving it.

Furth: For Piaget, "primordial" means what is in the child. That seems to make it at least a little bit more amenable to consensus.

Scott: The crib is close to the bed. One parent finds the crib too close and the other finds it too far away. The six-month old child seems, for reasons that are not quite clear, to sleep better when it's there than when it's anywhere else. What are we to say about the child and the two parents? I don't think that space is subjective. I don't think that the term "subjective" is adequate to describe what we're saying. I do believe that there is the experience of the space that is the child and the experience of the space that is this or that adult. They are both experiences of what we are not yet fully prepared to give an account of — namely an account of what we call space. The term "primordial" is not appropriate for either what adults experience or what the child experiences. Space is that by virtue of which we are near and far as children and as adults. I don't think that either the traditional empiricist, objective language nor the idealistic, subjective language is adequate to account for how we are in common together.

Furth: But eventually we don't talk about near and far anymore. We use numbers, and then near and far are meaningless. Only insofar as you have personal relations can you call it closeness. I don't think you could call it space.

Scott: I'm not trying to talk only about personal relations. No. "Near" and "far" name something. It doesn't go away when I become abstract.

Furth: Near? Far?

Scott: I'm just saying that "near" and "far" are not basically or primordially categories that apply to subjectivity.

Welton: How do you . . . methodologically . . . get at that? That's the question. How do you get at the primordial if you don't want to set Piaget aside?

Scott: I don't want to set Piaget aside.

Welton: At least on this question you find him limited. Do you want to extend Piaget in some sense? Or do you want to use a different kind of approach? What kind of method are you going to use?

Scott: The first step of such a method would be to provide an account of the experience of space in which no account can be absolute. If we have a method which relativizes the perspective such that for the method it becomes absolute, then we are developing an intelligence that is not solely defined by the method itself. This is the most difficult move right now for me and for most of us at this particular time. We tend to identify knowledge with rigorous method, which strikes me as fundamentally wrong. What is beyond that in terms of space? I believe that space is a commonality and that we do not now have a language that is able to communicate commonalities except in terms of subjective or objective structures. The goal or the *telos* of that kind of method would be to be able to speak of space without talking about subjective or objective postures . . . a non-posturing kind of knowledge. I think that it is accomplished in certain forms of poetry, which I would not want to call knowledge. But that envisagement is in our society. It's in our culture. The envisagement is; but usually when we move toward it, we start talking again in terms of subjective capacities or in terms of objective things as if we were not there at all. Neither of those moves is correct. When my wife feels too close and I feel too far, what is it that is too close, too far and just right? It is very difficult to describe and that seems odd. We can say it abstractly. We can say it metrically. We can say it psychologically. But in all those cases, it is a perspective upon something that is none of the three. Now how do we say space?

Welton: This example certainly coincides nicely with what you were trying to bring out last night about the necessity of introducing the ontological question.

Scott: Or of recognizing the ontological question which we have already introduced.

Welton: Okay. You would want to say then, as you did last night, that this is completely missing in Piaget. Obviously, it isn't.

Scott: Well. It is virtually missing from most methodologies which most of us use most of the time. Piaget is exemplary in that regard. What I find very interesting in Piaget is the combination of a high degree of discursive abstractions and at the same time a basic interactionist view of the world. That makes the conflict that I'm trying to articulate sharper in Piaget than in many. But it is still a conflict which I find deeply distorting of an effort to know what is there.

Casey: The further problem with this is that to ask that question or to know what is there or to know what space is are really adult questions. And I really think that it is a Kantian question. Heidegger and Gadamer are perfectly Kantian in this respect. They are asking for the fundamental ground of experience called space in this case.

Scott: That's true.

Casey: And even if it is not subject to rigorous formulations, to schemes and categories and so forth, it is still the same *adult* question.

Furth: We must ask adult questions because the infant doesn't ask questions.

Scott: Right. But we don't ask about adult realities. We ask about space. We don't ask about child realities. We ask about space.

Furth: There is no child category because we adults are the ones who categorize. If you are looking for some primordial category which is somehow in the child, you are asking for the impossible. As soon as you ask a question, you must ask an adult question.

Scott: Space is not a category. That is the point that I'm trying to make.

Furth: But I don't think that question is in the child's mind.

Casey: No. I don't think Charles Scott is claiming that the question is in the child's mind. He was implying that the conception might be in the child's experience.

Scott: No. I want to say that the child and the adult are in common in being and space. The questions we ask are adult questions. The categories we have are adult categories. But space is neither the question nor the category nor an object of the question. Space is necessarily that which we address.

Casey: I think that the very notion of something that we can address is an adult thing.

Scott: Anything that we can address in an adult way is the object of an adult experience. I can see that. But I don't think that it comes into existence by virtue of the adult address. What is the nature of this existence that can be addressed by the adult and the child in a non-addressing way?

Furth: But you cannot address in a non-addressing way. You are as a philosopher and a scientist . . .

Scott: No. I said that the child could be *in* in a non-addressing way. You're right about me. The child and I are in space and time.

Furth: Yes, but you are not satisfied with calling it space.

Scott: I don't mind the word but I sure have trouble understanding the reality.

Welton: With that, maybe we should give some thought to the reality of breaking for an adult lunch.

PIAGET AND FREUD ON CHILDHOOD MEMORY

Edward S. Casey

To attempt to bring together Piaget and Freud on the subject of memory may seem a foolhardy venture. Indeed, to bring together two such disparate figures on *any* topic may well appear misguided in view of the gulf that separates them. Although Piaget underwent a brief psychoanalysis as a young adult and even presented a paper on symbolic thinking in the child at the International Congress of Psychoanalysis in 1922 (a paper in which Freud himself showed interest), he assumed a critical stance toward Freud's work from the very beginning — claiming that its "theoretical conceptions require a general overhaul."[1] This overhaul is undertaken in *Play, Dreams, and Imitation in Childhood*, in which Freud's topographic conception of the unconscious is rejected in favor of a matrix of "affective schemes" that lie at the basis of symbol formation. Much more generally, Freud's stress on the mind's self-diremptive and self-deceiving character is replaced in Piaget by a cool vision of its organizing and self-regulating capacities. Primary process thereby gives way to secondary process, and it is all too tempting to think of Piaget as a purely "cognitive" psychologist of only remote relevance to the emotional and dynamic concerns of psychoanalysts. As if to acknowledge this very disparity, there is not a single reference to Piaget in the twenty-four volumes of *The Complete Psychological Works of Sigmund Freud.*[2]

When it comes to memory, the differences between the two figures seem only to loom larger. First, there is the striking fact that Freud's preoccupation with memory occurred during the earliest years of psychoanalysis (roughly the period 1893-1899) and that the prominent place of memory in these years was soon usurped by phantasy in Freud's thinking. Piaget, in

63

contrast, by and large neglects memory in his early work—only several brief pages treat it in *Plays, Dreams and Imitation in Childhood*, although this book focusses on the very period in which evocative memory first arises—and it is only near the end of his career, only some ten years ago in fact, that Piaget (in collaboration with Bärbel Inhelder) devoted a major work to the subject: *Memory and Intelligence*. What impressed Freud first intrigues Piaget last.

But there is a second and deeper difference between the two authors in regard to memory, specifically childhood memory. While both underline the significance of such memory—indeed, can claim to be the two primary discoverers of its most deeply veiled structures—each nonetheless takes toward it a resolutely different stance. Freud concerns himself most with the *fate* of early childhood memories, their vicissitudes in the adolescent and the adult, for whom it is a matter of memories *of* childhood; and he is most struck by the imperfection of these memories, especially by the fact that entire periods of childhood are subject to a nearly total amnesia (what do you remember of your life before, say, six years of age?) and that many memories which purport to be of childhood events before this point turn out to be misleading "screen memories," that is, complex commixtures of memory and phantasy that cover over (hence the term *Deckerinnerungen*) what really happened in our formative years. As Freud says skeptically:

> It may indeed be questioned whether we have any memories at all *from* our childhood: memories *relating to* our childhood may be all that we possess. Our childhood memories show us our earliest years not as they were but as they appeared at the later periods when the memories were aroused. (*SE* III, 322)

Piaget, on the other hand, is concerned not with surviving memories of childhood but with memories *in* childhood: with their precise mode of formation and intrinsic characteristics.[3] The rationale for this restriction of focus is not that adult memory is tenuous or treacherous but that in adults "mental functions (in general) have become too complex to be grasped by the subject's consciousness."[4] It is better, therefore, to return to a prior point where there is still a chance of comprehending how such a complicated function as memory operates.

Given such differences, both general and specific, between Piaget and Freud, I might seem to have rendered this paper impossible, or at least unpromising, from the very start. Yet real as these differences are, they do not begin to tell the whole story. Alongside the disparities are profound affinities between the two thinkers: affinities which exist at both of the levels of comparison just sketched out. At the more general level, it is evident, first of all, that Piaget·and Freud both achieve their most original and telling insights by privileging childhood as an arena of research: each tries to take much more seriously than previous investigators "the mental life of children, which we adults no longer understand and whose fullness and delicacy of feeling we have in consequence so greatly underestimated" (*SE* XIII, 99). We need only substitute "thought" for "feeling" in this statement from *Totem and Taboo* to win assent from Piaget. Nevertheless, and secondly, Freud was much more of a cognitive psychologist than meets the casual eye, as his intricate theory of thinking in the "Project for a Scientific Psychology" attests. We might also notice that, for all the emphasis on emotional re-living in psychoanalytic therapy — "recollection without affect almost invariably produces no result" in the celebrated dictum of *Studies on Hysteria* — the conception of affect is in fact one of the weakest parts of Freudian metapsychology. Piaget, for his part, has more to say about affect and emotion than is usually supposed, at one point even placing affective and intellectual schemes on a par with each other.[5] And, as for the topographic model of mind, Freud had himself long since questioned this by the time Piaget attacked it, adopting instead a "structuralist" model that in its emphasis on functions (especially ego functions) is reminiscent of Piaget's own insistence on psychical organizations and systems. Not only is the unconscious now regarded as a system of relationships (and not merely as a repository of repressed content), but the autonomy of the ego, its inherent tendency to seek an equilibrium not unlike Piaget's "equilibration," is increasingly stressed in Freud's later works.

But my concern here is much more with the second, more specific, level of comparison: that involving memory. For I am convinced that at this level the two figures are more continuous with each other than their most salient divergences lead us to think. To begin with, Freud is not uninterested in the way in which early memories are laid down, especially those of a traumatic nature, for he recognizes in these memories the germ of all later psychopathology. Exactly how they are formed, or misformed, becomes of vital interest in psychoanalysis, which cannot afford to consider childhood memories from the adult's position alone.[6] And Piaget, conversely, seeks more than a theory of memory as it arises in childhood; as the General Conclusion to *Memory and Intelligence* makes clear, it is on the basis of this delimited theory that one can go on to obtain insight into the nature of adult memory as well.[7] Just as Freud is less obsessed with affect and Piaget with cognition than we might assume, so the former views memory in a less adultomorphic and the latter in a less infantomorphic manner than we might guess.

Yet there is still another, more particular, way in which Freud and Piaget converge on the topic of memory, and it is to a discussion of this other aspect that the remainder of my study will be devoted. This convergence dawned upon me recently in presenting a talk on Freud's view of memory to a group of psychoanalysts. The next section of the present paper will retrace my steps and show the impasse to which I was led at that time. From there I shall turn to a detailed look at Piaget's theory of memory regarded as a possible way out of the impasse.

Part I

So Freud first; and I want to begin with a consideration of the case of the Wolf-man. The details of the early history of the Wolf-man (otherwise known only by his initials 'S.P.'), details first written down by Freud in 1914 after the Wolf-man had been in analysis with him for four years, are both too complex and too familiar to call for recounting here. (Freud himself summarizes these at *SE* XVII, 121.) Let me single out just two events in this history, though these are the ones which most concerned and fascinated Freud himself: the "wolf dream" and the observation of the primal scene. The Wolf-man mentioned the dream early in the analysis, and its compelling character made both him and Freud suspect that something of major magnitude lay concealed in it. The dream itself occurred when the Wolf-man was just turning four; a close analysis of its manifest content — especially the terrifying immobility of the wolves stationed in the tree and their fixed staring at the dreamer — led Freud to assume that the event from which it stemmed and which it represented (by reversal) was the Wolf-man's witnessing of the primal scene at the age of one and a half: the wolves' immobility was a cover for the violent motions of his parents in intercourse, their staring at him was in fact *his* staring at his parents in the act, and the wolves' bushy tails signified castration via a story about a tail-less wolf told to the young S.P. by his grandfather. Now, the primal scene experience was never recollected as such by the Wolf-man. Just as hysterics had earlier denied remembering an original trauma even though they were quite convinced of its existence,[8] so the Wolf-man could never admit to a definite recollection of the momentous scene that alone seemed to make sense of his shattered psyche. Far from being discouraged, Freud was only strengthened in his belief that such scenes are not normally recollected but must be *reconstructed* in analysis: "so far as my experience hitherto goes," he writes, "these scenes from infancy are not reproduced during the treatment as recollections, they are the products of [re]construction" (*SE* XVII, 50-1).

The result is that at the very nub of the Wolf-man's analysis, we discover all three of the main forms of memory which are operative in the analytical situation: *recollection* (of the wolf dream), *repetition* (of the primal scene by this dream), and *reconstruction* (of the primal scene itself). We also detect a basic pattern of at least two memories or memory-elements and two repetitions: a pattern that emerges in other case histories of Freud's as well. The wolf dream is explicitly considered a form of memory by Freud, and the ensuing wolf phobia (which set in immediately after the fateful dream) treats wolves as "mnemic symbols." And, just as the dream repeats the primal scene, so the wolf phobia repeats the dream. But this minimal pattern is complicated in the present case by the fact that the symptom itself belongs to the past and is recollected from the vantage point of the analytic situation. In contrast with certain other cases, there is no longer a coincidence or overlap between the period of symptomatology and the period of analysis. We may encapsulate this particular sequence in the following formula, where 'P' stands for the present psychoanalytic situation, ' $\rightleftharpoons$ ' for repetition, and 'M_1' through 'M_3' for the memory-elements dealt with in that situation (in this instance, the primal scene, the wolf dream, and the wolf phobia, respectively):

$$\left[\left[M_1 \rightleftharpoons M_2\right] \rightleftharpoons M_3\right] \rightleftharpoons P$$

Now, '$M_1 \rightleftharpoons M_2$', the content of the innermost brackets, functions as an essential nuclear unit. Without at least two closely connected memory-elements at its disposal, the psychoanalytic situation at 'P' could not connect insightfully with the patient's past—in contrast with the ordinary, non-analytic situation, in which a single consciously recollected memory suffices to bring the past back before us meaningfully (for example, as an object of nostalgic contemplation or as a point of departure for future endeavors). In this light, Breuer's cathartic method, which Freud tried to practice but soon abandoned and which aims at reviving a single traumatic event in hallucinatory vivacity, can be seen as mistakenly modelled on everyday remembering, replacing a diphasic approach to the past with the hope for a uniphasic recapture. But it must also be emphasized that '$M_1 \rightleftharpoons M_2$' is only a *minimal* unit. The very example of the Wolf-man forces us to supplement this unit by adding a third memory-component, 'M_3.' In fact, still further supplementation is required, for there is no fixed limit to the number of extra memory-elements that can be added onto the series whose nucleus is '$M_1 \rightleftharpoons M_2$.' These subsequent elements may be in the form of explicit recollections, reconstructions, or blind repetitions (e.g., new dreams, new symptoms, actings out and various transference phenomena). These may be designated by 'M_n' and the basic formula completed as follows:

$$\left\{ \cdots \left[\left[M_1 \rightleftharpoons M_2 \right] \rightleftharpoons M_3 \right] \rightleftharpoons \cdots \rightleftharpoons M_n \right\} \rightleftharpoons P$$

Central to Freud's revolution in psychology was his refusal to accept the Aristotelian paradigm of efficient causality as a valid model for memory. He found, from the very beginning of his inquiries into psychopathology, that a memory is more than a copy or mimetic residue of a past event — that, far from being the passive simulacrum of this event, it has its own causal efficacy, an efficacy which may exceed that inherent in the original event itself, thereby contravening the ancient assumption that there must be at least as much reality in an efficient cause as in its effect. Already in the *Studies on Hysteria* Freud asserts that "in every analysis of a case of hysteria based on sexual traumas we find that impressions from the pre-sexual period which produced no effect on the child [at the time] attain traumatic power at a later date *as memories"* (*SE* II, 133; my italics). This statement is remarkable for its audacious claims that: (1) certain causes (here "impressions from the pre-sexual period") do not exert a significant effect (i.e., have "traumatic power") until a later moment, at which point they are no longer in existence themselves; and (2) this effect is exerted by memories, which must therefore be more than pale copies of their causes. In other words, the power resides *in the memories and not in the impressions:* just the opposite of what Aristotle, Descartes, Hume and the commonsensical thinking that reflects their views would hold.

In his bold essay of 1896, "Heredity and the Aetiology of the Neuroses" (in which the word "psychoanalysis" first appeared), Freud maintained that the memory of an early sexual trauma acts as the *specific cause* of hysteria — where by "specific cause" is meant neither a general precondition nor a "concurrent" or precipitating cause, but an indispensable factor uniquely suited to bring about a given effect. Freud reasoned that the specific cause of hysteria does not lie in particular childhood experiences, not even in seduction (much as Freud was tempted to see in this the root of all neurosis), for too many people report having had such experiences and yet do not become hysterics. If nevertheless these experiences are pathogenic — that is to say, genuine preconditions — then it must be their *memory* that acts as the specific causal agent directly giving rise to hysteria. Such a memory "will display a power which was completely lacking from the event itself. [It] will operate as though it were a contemporary event."[9] Therefore, a memory, the effect of an event, *itself becomes an event,* and is the specifically determinative event in the genesis of hysteria. Freud concludes the essay by remarking that:

> So far as I can see, this awakening of a sexual memory after puberty, when the event itself has happened at a time long before that period, forms the only psychological instance of the immediate effect of a *memory* surpassing that of an actual [i.e., external] event . . . In this way we arrive at a very complex psychical problem, but one which, properly appreciated, promises to throw a vivid light on the most delicate questions of psychical life. (*SE* III, 154; his italics)

The problem may not have a solution yet, but it does have a name: "deferred action" (*Nachträglichkeit*). This term appears for the first time in the "Project for a Scientific Psychology" of 1895, in a discussion of the case of Emma:

> Now this case is typical of repression in hysteria. We invariably find that a memory is repressed which has only become a trauma by *deferred action*. (*SE* I, 356; his italics)

The *fact* of deferred action by memory may be taken as established — as is illustrated by the very example of Emma, whose memory of an early assault operated in a deferred fashion by making a later scene of being laughed at in a clothing store the precipitating cause of a phobia about entering shops when alone. But *how* does such deferred action work? What is its inner mechanism?

Freud's only attempt at an extended explanation, given in Part II of the "Project" and intriguingly entitled "Determinants of the *Proton Pseudos* (False Premiss)," centers on the way in which the ego is misled by an apparently tame memory of a childhood scene and fails to erect a defense against it — thereby allowing the memory to discharge its concealed and pent-up affect: the ego, acting on a false premiss, "permits a primary process [i.e., a release of affect] because it did not expect one" (SE I, 358).

Ingenious as this explanation may be, it leaves too many questions unanswered. How is it that the affect goes unnoticed until the precise moment described? Why is memory the privileged vehicle of its deviously delayed discharge? In what way does this discharge represent an *action* and not merely a mechanical response? Above all, is the deferred action of memory adequately conceived in terms of release of affect, or is something else involved?

That something else *is* involved is at least hinted at by Freud in another remark he makes à propos of Emma:

> Here we have the case of a memory arousing an affect which it did not arouse as an experience, because in the meantime the change [brought about] in puberty had made possible *a different understanding* of what was remembered. (*SE* I, 356; my italics)

The something else in question, and a more adequate conception of deferred action itself, is contained in the seemingly innocuous phrase "a different understanding." It is revealing that in almost every mention which Freud makes of deferred action, from the early case of Katharina to that of the Wolf-man, the word "understanding" is employed as an explanatory term — whereas the adroit but affect-oriented explanation just summarized is never again invoked. Why is this? What is it about "understanding" that makes this single term more illuminating than the much more intricate reasoning of the *proton pseudos*?

Here we may take a clue from Aristotle, who said with disarming simplicity that "memory is of the past."[10] For memory to be of the past is for it necessarily to involve understanding. This is due to the fact that the past presents itself in a precarious mixture of presence and absence — presence in the form of the memory-image, absence in the form of the original experience intended in and by the image. This experience, to which the rememberer ascribes the predicate "past," is brought back to mind by means of the memory-image. Yet if, contra Aristotle, this image is not a mental facsimile of the experience — "memory," said Aristotle in his short treatise on the subject, "is the having of an image regarded as a copy of that of which it is an image"[11] — then we can never be certain in a given case of remembering as to: (a) how accurately the experience is being represented by the image, which may distort it to suit present purposes, conscious or unconscious; or (b) whether what we take to be the past experience *was* an experience and not the product of a retrospective illusion. Thus the uneasy blend of absence and presence in memory leads readily to the sort of skepticism concerning the validity of memory-claims which we have seen Freud profess in his essay on "Screen Memories." But by the same token it also leads to an awareness that the past in its very precariousness calls for understanding. It is the sort of thing that must be understood and not, say, perceived or even retrodicted. But what kind of understanding does it call for?

Let us return to the Wolf-man and particularly to an important passage which Freud inexplicably relegates to a footnote:

[The wolf dream] is simply another instance of deferred action. At the age of one and a half the child receives an impression to which he is unable to react adequately; he is only able to *understand* it and to be moved by it when the impression is revived in him at the age of four [i.e., in the wolf dream]; and only twenty years later, during the analysis, is he able to grasp with his conscious mental processes what was then going on in him. (*SE* XVII, 45 n; my italics)

This is Freud's first acknowledgement that deferred action can occur *before* puberty — that it is not only "the retardation of puberty [that] makes possible posthumous primary processes" (*SE* I, 359). Deferred action can occur long before this, not because the infantile ego can be foiled in the manner described in the "Project," but because the understanding of an initial trauma and the release of affect it occasions may arise at a much earlier age than Freud had previously allowed: as a four-year old, the Wolf-man is able to understand an experience which he could not comprehend as a one-and-a-half-year old. But what sort of understanding is this?

To make matters still more difficult, it is an understanding that occurs in
the form of a dream — which is to say, as a form of memory, for dreaming
in Freud's view is "another kind of remembering, though one that is subject to the conditions that rule at night and to the laws of dream-
formation" (*SE* XVII, 51). In fact, the wolf dream is both an act of
understanding *and* an act of remembering; and *it is an instance of deferred action by virtue of being both of these together.* The primal scene has
had its deferred effect not just in being recalled at a later point but in being recalled with understanding (albeit a symbolically disguised understanding: an understanding unclear to itself). But, once again, what more
exactly *is* this understanding? Freud himself offers only the barest of hints,
alluding to "an advance in intellectual development" which renders what
was formerly "unassimilable" to the ego comprehensible to it.[12]

In short, we have reached the impasse to which I referred in my opening remarks, since we are at a loss to say what precise sort of progress in
understanding would make the Wolf-man's memory at age four so crucial-
ly different from what it was at one and a half.[13] Hence Freud's most
famous and significant case is left dangling — unless and until we can find a
way to make sense of deferred understanding in memory.

Part II

The sense is supplied by Piaget's theory of the development of memory in
childhood, to which I now turn. In reading *Memory and Intelligence,* I
have been impressed by the frequency with which Piaget expressly links
memory and understanding as co-ordinate terms.[14] Let me cite several
representative passages:

> We found that the memory of our subjects was very closely bound up with
> their level of understanding. (19)
>
> What the memory retains is chiefly what the subject has understood. (201)
>
> Durable remembrance is not possible unless it is based on true under-
> standing. (261)
>
> Our readers by now have come to take it for granted that our subjects will
> only remember those aspects of the model [presented to them] which they
> have fully understood. (116)

Moreover, unlike Freud, Piaget goes on to specify the nature of the relationship between memory and understanding. First of all, he shows that
given levels of achievement or performance in remembering a particular

object or event are almost invariably correlated with various levels of understanding of the same object or event. This correlation is established in detail in each of the twenty experiments reported in *Memory and Intelligence*, typically by demonstrating the close correspondence between four or five levels of remembrance and the same number of levels of understanding. This does not mean that what is remembered is *confined* to what has been understood — extraneous, un-understood details may sometimes be recalled — but it does mean that the main and most important part of what we remember reflects, and is a function of, what we have grasped in understanding,[15] even if it is an understanding that is not yet explicit or thematic and that has to be determined by separate testing procedures.

Secondly, Piaget clarifies the character of the relationship in question by interpreting the notion of "levels of understanding" in a quite specific way: as modes of operative intelligence. By this is meant intelligence guided by schemes (*schèmes*), *a priori* structures of action and knowledge. Much like Kant's "transcendental schemata" — which belong precisely to "understanding" (*Verstand*) in the Kantian system and which serve to link pure concepts and sensible intuitions by a "universal procedure . . . of providing an image [Piaget's *schéma*] for a concept"[16] — Piagetian schemes are procedures for assimilating experiences and understanding them in their generality. As such, they are the basis for accommodation to *new* experiences, where "accommodation," like Kant's empirical schema, is always tied to something discrete and particular: in Kant's example, to five actually perceived dots (. . . . .) rather than to the number five.[17] Memory, like any cognitive activity, is always both assimilatory and accommodative at once: the former in its pure schematic basis, the latter in the figurative component that may be of a perceptual, imitative, or imagistic character.

It is in terms of its mode of assimilation, its exact kind of schematizing activity, that the operative level of a particular memory is determined. Such activity can range from the merely habitual (especially characteristic of the sensori-motor period) to the abstract and logical at the stage of formal operations. The specific schemes operative in memory, however, fall for the most part between these two extremes. We can see this by a brief consideration of the three main sorts of memory as they are distinguished by Piaget:

    (a) *recognition:* this is solidary with perception, occurs in the presence of the object remembered, and makes use of "perceptual indices" in the object, assimilating these to sensori-motor schemes ranging from reflex reactions to complex classifications of perceptual objects.

(b) *reconstruction:* Piaget insists on the importance of this neglected mnemonic mode, which bridges the gap between Bergson's two types of memory (habitual and recollective)[18]; one can as legitimately remember by non-habitual, reconstructive actions as by perceptual recognition or memory-images: e.g., in putting together again a model formerly displayed intact (a frequent exercise in Piaget's experiments); thus reconstruction is to be defined as "the intentional reproduction of a particular action and of its results" (*MI*, 393).

(c) *recall (évocation):* like reconstruction, this occurs in the absence of the model or original experience; but it is achieved by memory-images or words rather than by bodily actions; these images or words serve as representations of the recollected content.

The three primary types of memory (and the ten corresponding subtypes, whose existence indicates that there is development within each major type)[19] are related to each other within the general framework of intellectual development, especially its first two stages of sensori-motor and representational functioning. For if recognition is rooted in the sensori-motor period, reconstruction lies on the borderline between this period and that of representation (in which the "semiotic function" emerges), while recall originates entirely in this latter stage. In particular, reconstruction is a form of deferred imitation by bodily movements of a given object or event; and when imitation becomes not only deferred but *internalized* as well, mental imagery, the chief basis of recall, becomes possible. Such imagery is symbolic or "motivated" in the Saussurean sense of involving a resemblance between signifier and signified: the memory-image is a quasi-pictorial representation of the remembered scene.

Piaget is insistent, however, that a memory-image is never a strict *reproduction* of such a scene, as theories of engrams and memory traces imply. For the memory-image is itself a signifier, not merely a mental picture, and its *signifié* ("significate" in the English translation) is not the originally experienced scene *per se* but the scene as soliciting the schemes by which it was assimilated and thus understood in the first place.[20] At no point, therefore, can we say that recall (or, for that matter, recognition or reconstruction) is "limited to the reproduction of figurative inputs; rather, such inputs [are] subordinated at all levels to the operative schemes governing their assimilation."[21] Such schemes actively structure both the memory-image and that of which it is an image. Thus we have come a long way from Aristotle's copy theory, with its model of passively reproductive replication. Piaget's model, by contrast, is resolutely activist, and it is so to the exact extent that it privileges the schematic over the pictorial element in memory.

As actively schematizing in character, memory is *ipso facto* a form of intelligence, for "the schemes utilized by memory are [all] borrowed from intelligence" (*MI*, 382). This is not to say that memory is a mere tributary or contingent outgrowth of intelligence. Piaget emphasizes that intelligence needs memory as a means of representing and vivifying the past, as supplying "particular and concrete models which it needs in order to engage in constructive activities" (*MI*, 390), and as leading to the greater differentiation of schemes themselves: "the greater the number of objects and details retained by a memory, the more [a given] scheme must be differentiated into sub-systems."[22] Yet even if there is a "mutual dependence"[23] of memory and intelligence, it remains the case that intelligence is the more fundamental term. As Piaget says at many points, "the conservation of memories rests on the conservation of schemes" (for example, *MI*, 390), and schemes, strictly speaking, belong to intelligence. It is for this reason that in Piaget's conception of memory the operative or schematic aspect prevails over the figurative aspect, which is always tied down to a localized and particular object or event in the past.[24] Of course, as Aristotle has reminded us, memory is *of* the past, and it is therefore always figurative in some fashion. It can even be said to be the figurative aspect of the general schematism of *all* intelligence.[25] But it remains the case that it depends on intelligence more than intelligence depends on it, and in the end operativity predominates over figurativity. And if this is so, we should expect the structure and evolution of memory to mirror the structure and evolution of intelligence itself. This is precisely Piaget's leading thesis: "the development of memory with age is the history of gradual organizations closely dependent on the structuring activities of intelligence" (*MI*, 381). The result is that memory is "a constant restructuring process" (*MI*, 381), a form of "permanent reorganization" (378-9). How this is so we may observe in the following experiments excerpted from *Memory and Intelligence:*

Experiment #1

Let us begin with the simplest, and yet also the most striking, of the experiments reported in the book, namely, remembering a single serial configuration of rods arranged in gradually increasing heights. To construct this model, represented in stages III-IV of Fig. 1, one must be capable of employing the operative scheme of seriation, which involves an activity of double co-ordination (i.e., realizing that any non-terminal rod is both smaller than its successors and larger than its predecessors). Now, the fundamental question being raised in this experiment is whether the memory of such a figure is based on the possession of this operation or, rather, on the purely perceptual aspect of the model—in this instance, a "good Gestalt" that would seem to facilitate memory at any age, but especially in childhood with its fabled capacity for eidetic imagery.

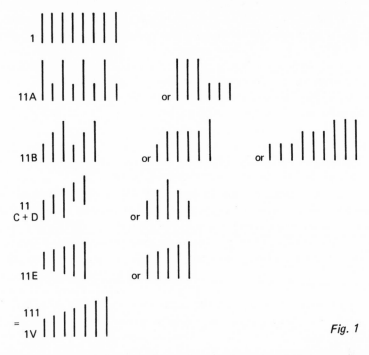

Fig. 1

The first result of the experiment is that there is a definite sequence of levels in remembering the model (where these levels are determined by drawings of the model from memory or by tracing out its form with a finger) *and* that these levels correspond to the stages by which the scheme of simple seriation develops on its own and without being explicitly remembered. This "synchronism between operational stages and memory levels" (*MI*, 38) is evident in the sequence of levels in Fig. 1: at first (at ages 3-4 years), there is a memory involving no attempt at seriation at all (I); next, at ages 4-5 years, we see a number of intermediate steps involving various imperfect groupings of pairs and triads (II A); and then (starting at age 5 years) there are various attempts at establishing a seriated form (II B, C, D, and E) before success is achieved at 6-8 years of age with levels III-IV.[26] These same stages are passed through by children who are being tested for their operational capacity alone, and thus we have a first illustration of the way in which memory and intelligence (and hence understanding) are closely correlated.

But there is a second, and still more telling, result. The foregoing result was based on memories of the model after a lapse of one week. If, however, the same subjects were asked to remember the model after a period of seven to eight months, in 74 per cent of the group as a whole and in 90 per cent of those from 5-8 years of age, there was a marked *improvement* in their memory drawings! The progress, moreover, is all the more significant in that it normally proceeds in a regular manner from one memory level to the next, without leaping over intermediate levels. It is as if we can see the development of memory before our very eyes.

The most plausible interpretation of both sets of results is that advances in memory are tied to advances in the operational scheme to which the model of the series has been assimilated: how else could one remember this series better after eight months than after one week? The initially preoperational scheme has become more fully operational in the interim, and the memory-image attached to this scheme as its signifier changes so as to reflect the change in the scheme itself.[27] The evolving scheme, then, is the critical factor and not the initial perception of the model; despite the good Gestalt of the latter, it was not perceived accurately, as the irregularities of the memory-drawings done after one week suggest; nor does it make sense to say that the initial perception somehow evolves in and of itself: if anything, we should expect deterioration over time, as in a theory of memory as the simple storage of perceptual data. Hence Piaget can conclude as follows:

> The memory of the series [in question] is not the perceptual and imaginal reproduction [*décalque*] of the series as such, conceived as an object wholly independent of the subject (and thus unlikely to be transformed in the course of eight months), but rather . . . the memory of the series is the image or representative of a scheme which has itself evolved.[28]

Experiment #2

This is again surprisingly simple, yet just as surprisingly significant. Children of ages 5-9 years were asked to remember a model composed of two rows of four match sticks each, A and A' in Fig. 2:

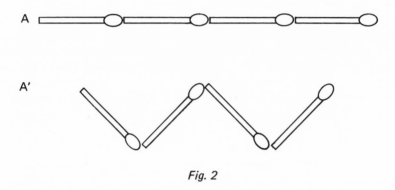

Fig. 2

In the perception and memory of this figure, at least two schemes are at play and, until the age of 9 years, *in conflict with each other.* On the one hand, there is a scheme of numerical correspondence, by means of which the child correlates the number of matches in row A with those in A'. On the other hand, there is a scheme of spatial conservation, according to which the respective lengths of A and A' are seen to be equal. But since this latter scheme lags behind in development (it is fully operative only at 8-9 years of age), its pre-operational form, based on centration upon end-points rather than upon length proper, prevails. The pre-operational child, confronted with the model and correctly noting the numerical correspondence of the matches, concludes that the two sets of end-points must also correspond. This is a momentarily satisfying, if illusory, solution to the conflict in question, and leads to memory drawings of Types 2 and 3 in Fig. 3, wherein we see efforts to equalize end-points whether at the expense of numerical correspondence (Type 2) or not (Type 3).

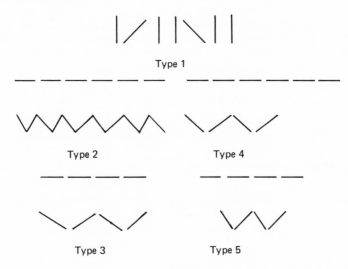

Fig. 3

The primarily figurative solution of Types 2 and 3 is preceded by Type 1 drawings, where the matches are merely arranged in vertical rows, indicating that in the 5 year olds who remember the model in this way (and only 5 year olds do so), there is not yet an incompatibility between schemes because these latter have not yet developed to the point where conflict is possible. By the ages of 6 and 7 years, in contrast, the conflict is at full height: twenty-five of fifty-two six year olds produced figures of Type 2. Only at 9 years is the conflict resolved and a correct remembrance rendered as in Type 5. Consequently, "the progress of the schemes serves first to exacerbate the conflict before it eventually resolves it" (*MI*, 81), and in contradistinction to the first experiment (which Piaget admits to be almost "too good to be true" [*MI*, 50], we witness stagnation and even regression.[29] This disparity of results should not, however, mislead us: the very lack of improvement in the present case is itself a sign of the influence of schematic factors, which are no less operative here than previously. In both instances, there is an assimilation of the model to schemes, but the incompatibility between the relevant schemes to which the match sticks are assimilated lands children of ages 6-7 years in a "systematic quandary" from which they attempt to extricate themselves by the false (but predictable) memories of Types 2 and 3. As Piaget remarks, "the use of schemes cuts both ways: it leads to errors no less than to the adequate organization and consolidation of memory" (*MI*, 341).

There is a further twist to this experiment which is worth mentioning. If the lower row A' is reshaped into a more pronounced 'W' form, the conflict in question will suddenly vanish and better mnemonic results will be produced. Why? Because the more acute form reminds the child of such familiar shapes as a row of housetops, a mountain range, or the letter 'W' itself. He will spontaneously assimilate the new form to the schemes appropriate to these latter figures. Since the new schemes do not conflict with the scheme for row A, the separate and correct memory of *both* rows is facilitated, as in the right-hand portion of Fig. 4:

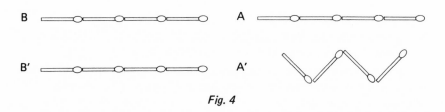

Fig. 4

And there is another twist to this twist: if two horizontal rows are now added to the left of A and A' respectively, conflict will be *reintroduced*, with a consequent regression in memories of the new figures. For the stress on numerical correspondence between the matches in B and B' serves to underscore the same correspondence between A and A', thereby inducing the subjects once more to make the end-points of the latter coincide in order to deal with this "scandalous state of affairs" (*MI*, 87).

A final avatar of this experiment is represented in Fig. 5, where the model to the left, being composed of a continuous line, masks the conflict between numerical and spatial schemes inherent in the model to the right. The consequence is that the continuous figure is remembered with much greater accuracy among 5-7 year olds, for whom the conflict in question is most acute when explicitly underscored as in the model on the right.[30]

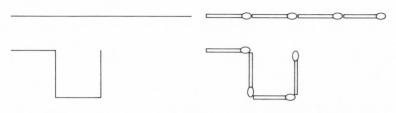

Fig. 5

This ingenious and somewhat sinuous experiment shows quite forcefully that the memory of the different models proffered cannot be construed as any simple copying or recording of perceptions. Rather than being explanatory of the memories obtained, the perceptions themselves are problematic, since at the pre-operational stage there does not seem to be a straightforward, unambivalent perception of the model: even memory drawings produced just one hour after the perception of the original model were distorted in the various manners discussed. If the child can be said generally to "produce the most faithful [memory-]image possible of what he has seen," it is nonetheless "an image that is more faithful to his thought than to his perception,"[31] that is, more faithful to his *understanding,* for the schemes subtending the child's thought and leading to distortions in his memory *are* his understanding of what he has seen and remembered.

Experiment #3

Here we are concerned with the memory of the models presented in Fig. 6 and 7 below. The first of these is structured by a double seriation of decreasing size and of changing color (here represented by varying striations and tonalities). Memories of it follow the now-familiar pattern of improvement with age, although progress is in this case more gradual (especially after six months) than with the simple seriation of the first experiment. This is just as we might guess, since we now have to do with a visual matrix involving the multiplicative co-ordination of two simultaneous seriations.[32] Still, by age 8 years, there is a "correct structuring of recall and reconstruction, due to the acquisition of the corresponding operational system, and not to simple figural [i.e., perceptual] influences which, as such, would have made themselves felt much earlier" (*MI*, 147).

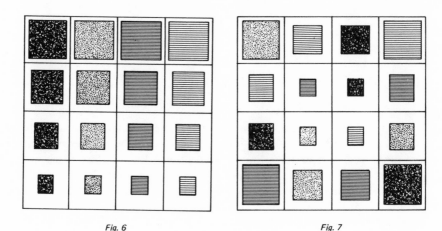

Fig. 6   Fig. 7

The second figure tells another story. It is strictly symmetrical and aesthetically more pleasing than the first figure — in other words, a better Gestalt and hence, one might think, more readily rememberable as such. But it is without operational significance for the children being tested, not being constructed by any specific operations within their grasp. Therein lies the catch, for it turns out that despite its Gestaltist virtues it is much more difficult for children to remember effectively. Wholly random memories persist in children up to 8 years of age, whereas this Type I response ceases at age 6 years in the case of the doubly seriated figure. Accurate memories begin to appear only at ages 9-10 years, and many subjects even at 12 years of age cannot successfully remember it after one week, much less after six months.[33]

At the same time, there is a notable effort on the part of certain children in the experiment to remember Fig. 7 in a form into which they have introduced their *own* improvised and quite imaginary seriations. As Piaget remarks, "here we have something like a search for, an implicit need of, serial order" (*MI*, 154). As in the comparable case reported later in *Memory and Intelligence* of a wholly incomprehensible causal process, the originally perceived figure does not link up with any available schemes, and there ensues a desperate compensatory attempt to organize the memory of it in *some* fashion, however inappropriately.[34] Once again, it is a matter of understanding — or rather, of the lack of it. Where otherwise (for example in the case of single or double seriation or even of the mismatched matches) the child can draw upon intact or developing schemes which, "being exercised outside the experimental situation and [thus] becoming more perfect, lead quite spontaneously to a [corrective] restructuring of certain memories," in the instance of Fig. 7 and of the incomprehensible causal process "the child is faced with a problem quite beyond his powers of understanding [since] he cannot invoke any [pertinent] schemes" (*MI*, 235).

Consider, finally, the contrasting case of a figure which, like the seriated squares of Fig. 6, involves a double classification but which is deliberately poorly represented — camouflaged, as it were. Despite a certain age-retardation effect in remembering this figure, memory after one week "corresponds almost exactly to the subjects' level of understanding" and after six months seven of thirty-four subjects made "clear progress" in their memory-drawings of it.[35] In these cases, what has happened is that the misleading figurative aspect has been overcome or overlooked so as to allow the schematic factor to come into operation: a quite convincing demonstration of the secondariness of perception and of the primacy of understanding. For such an inadequately represented figure to be recalled correctly, it *has* to be understood.[36]

Part III

Beyond their intrinsic interest, the upshot of these elegantly simple experiments is "ultra-clear" (to use Freud's expression): they "reveal the importance of mnemonic organizations in all age groups, and show that they develop as intelligence [itself] does" (*MI*, 381). Rather than a mere recording machine, memory is seen to be a "transformative organization," a successive *re*-organizing of its own contents by a process of "active and selective structuring" (*MI*, 378). This structuring occurs continuously and is not restricted to a given phase of memory-formation. As Piaget says emphatically, the schemes at work in memories are "active during retention and recall no less than during [their original] fixation" (*MI*, 383). Memory is not a matter of instantaneous encoding, followed by an equivalent act of decoding upon recall, as recent information-processing models have suggested. For *the code itself evolves* in the course of retention, and it evolves in accordance with the underlying schemes on which it depends for its very intelligibility.[37]

Piaget's dynamic conception of memory is also to be distinguished from two other competing models:

(a) First, there is the view of Pierre Janet that what we call memory is wholly a matter of retrospective narration ("*conduite du récit*") in which we construct past events in the present and *in the present alone*, that is, at the moment of recollection. This radical reconstructionist theory is placed in question by the fact that in some (and perhaps even in many) instances a specific mode of mnemonic inference intervenes *between* the original experience and its recall. A case in point is found precisely in the second experiment reported above: between the initial perception of the two rows (A and A') of matches in Fig. 2 and the mistaken memory that the rows had exactly equivalent end-points, there occurred an inference to the effect that 'if there are the same number of matches in each row, they must have the same end-points.' It is the latter clause alone that becomes the memory; the unrecalled inference, therefore, must have arisen at some point during retention.[38] And if this is so, Janet's thesis falls to the ground.

(b) Second, there is the view, which Piaget attributes to Freud and to Bergson, that memory consists altogether in retention—that "the entire past is recorded and conserved in the unconscious" (*MI*, 17) and conserved in such a way as never to change, even if our interpretations and uses of it may alter. On this view, the only changes are quantitative ones: we may retain more or less information, or forget more or less. But if the acquisition and extinction rates may thus vary, neither the content nor the mechanisms by which this content is remembered can change.[39] In opposition to this static, strictly conservationist model, Piaget argues that changes in memory are *qualitative* and affect both its content and its mechanisms. As we have just seen at some length, the very content and structure of memories alter with age; especially after intelligence enters the representational period, "successive pre-operational and operational structures . . . continually transform the organization of memory and provide the schematizations that modify its very adequacy and conservation" (*MI*, 380). Hence conservation or retention, far from being the *basis* of memory, is itself a *result* (and a constantly changing result) of the schematizing activity on which all phases of memory are founded. "Throughout our life," says Piaget, "we organize our memories and our vision of the past, conserving more or less the same material [to this extent, retention is not denied], but adding other elements capable of changing its significance and, above all, of changing our perspectives [on it]" (*MI*, 381).

Admirable and correct as this critique may be of a pure conservationist model, we must ask ourselves if this is indeed the model espoused by Freud — or even by Bergson, whose stress on the "virtuality" inherent in all memories prevents him from espousing any thesis of constant conservation.[40] But, Bergson aside, what about Freud? — It is true that in some of his early pronouncements Freud spoke of the "astonishing intactness" of memories recovered under hypnosis. But he soon abandoned hypnotic technique in favor of free association, in which the dramatic reappearance of long-forgotten scenes from childhood is much less frequent. And, even when such scenes do present themselves, they must be regarded with considerable skepticism, since any memory purporting to date from childhood is potentially a screen memory. (Lacan has claimed recently that *all* childhood memories are screened! Freud and Lacan would agree, I think, that any such memories should at least be *treated* as if they were screen memories, that is, a compromise formations comparable to dreams and symptoms.)[41] Now, even if only *some* of our childhood memories are screened, to admit this is tantamount to rejecting the "ultra-conservationist" view which Piaget (who admits that he deliberately refrains from calling this view "ultra-conservative") imputes to Freud; for it is to hold that memories are subject to infusions and transformations which preclude their retention or retrieval in a pristine form. Nor will it do to cite Freud's adhesion to the notion of "memory-trace" as evidence for his conservationism, since the very idea of *Erinnerungsspür* is highly equivocal in Freud's work and is even interpreted at one point as a *sign* — hence comparable to Piaget's own interpretation of the memory-trace as "a scheme in process of formation."[42]

There is an important passage at the very end of *Memory and Intelligence* in which Piaget reveals both his appreciation *and* his misunderstanding of Freud on the question of memory. In this passage, he first praises Freud for having detected the hidden and pervasive influence of the past (particularly the past of childhood) — "this was Freud's great discovery"[43] — and then adds in an apparent effort to correct or supplement this discovery:

On the other hand, the individual continuously reorganizes the past in his schemes (since they have obviously become modified by and adapted to

the present), and especially in his idea of this past, thus in his representation and his memory [of it]. (*MI*, 381)

Yet this statement is so far from being anti-Freudian that it can even be
said to be the point of view of Freud himself and to be his *second* great
discovery! For Freud too emphasizes the way in which we reorganize the
past to suit needs and wishes arising in the present. This retro-active
reshaping of the past from the perspective of the present is at work not only
in remembering as such (where it leads to amnesia, misremembering, *déjà
vu* experiences, etc., as well as to screen memories) but in *all* defensive
restructuring of past events, including neurotic symptoms (which distort
the past by denial, reversal, isolation, etc.), parapraxes, jokes, and dreams.

And dreams: in a footnote to the same passage, Piaget remarks that the
reorganization of the past by schemes at work in the present may occur by
"unconscious" or by "conscious" representation (MI, 381 n). Dreaming is
in fact an unconscious representation of past events in disguised and
distorted form. A dream modifies the structure of these events by its
mechanisms of condensation, displacement, and symbolization, changing
the presentation of the past so as to render it unrecognizable to the dreaming mind. As such, dreaming belongs to the semiotic function, and arises
(as Piaget himself has noted) at the same time as, and in the midst of, the
other activities by which this function is realized: deferred imitation, drawing, symbolic play, verbal language and mental imagery. But it is most
closely affiliated with that species of mental imagery which forms the basis
of evocative memory or recall: memory-images.[44] Just as these images supply the figurative factor in recall—its mode of accommodation to past
events in their concreteness and particularity—so dream-images effect the
figurative, or more exactly dis-figurative, restoration of repressed or
traumatic events. And if memory-images possess schemes—i.e.,
assimilatory elements that allow memory to become *knowledge* of the
past[45] and not only its invocation—so dream-images are more than images
alone but also serve as signs: as image-signs or what Freud explicitly calls a
form of "pictographic script" (*Bilderschrift*). Therefore, despite their
undeniably and often luxuriantly figurative character,[46] dreaming and
recall are both semiotically grounded, teaching us that there is no *schéma*
without a *schème*:[47] no figuration without schematization,[48] no picture
without a sign, no dream scene without a dream sense, no accommodation
to the past by memory-images without the assimilation by means of which
this past was first experienced and known. In short, we can say of dreams
what Piaget says of memory itself: "it is a form of organization which,

though mainly figurative, rests on the entire schematism of intelligence" (*MI*, 379).

On the basis of these remarks, we are at last in a better position to glimpse the significance of the wolf dream, which has been left dangling for too long. Freud's own final judgment is that "what sprang into activity that night out of the [young Wolf-man's] unconscious memory-traces was the picture of copulation between his parents" (*SE* XVII, 36). Now, it is not accidental that the night in question was the night before the Wolf-man's fourth birthday (as it was also the night before Christmas), and I point to this not because of the date as such but because of his age at the time: just turning 4 years of age, which is to say, in the very middle of the representational, pre-operational period of his life. Not only could the Wolf-man at this age dream symbolically, but he could remember *by* dreaming; his dream of wolves was "another kind of remembering" because direct recollection of the primal scene was too painful or too threatening. The wolf dream was the way, the only way acceptable to the child's ego, of remembering the traumatic event experienced at one and a half years of age, precisely the point at which the semiotic function first comes into being.

The primal scene thus acted in a deferred fashion, thanks to the emergence of the capacity for deferred imitation, which, internalized, makes both memory-images and dream-images possible.[49] Moreover, every deferred action reflects a deferred understanding.[50] The wolf dream is not only a belated and disguised picture of parental intercourse but embodies a belated understanding of what this intercourse implies or signifies — as is shown by the tellingly terrifying character by which it symbolizes castration, the price to be paid for having intercourse with one's father. As image and sign come together in the formation of every dream, so too do remembering and understanding; and every such conjunction is an instance of *Nachträglichkeit*. The wolf dream is a second trauma (it was, after all, a nightmare and led directly to a wolf phobia) that repeats the primary trauma in symbolic form, remembering it and understanding it in oneiric signs. The two traumas, thus linked, form the minimal psychopathic unit discussed earlier: '$M_1 \rightleftharpoons M_2$.' It needs to be stressed that 'M_2' can repeat 'M_1' by a variety of means — by explicit recollection, by reconstruction, but also (as in the present case) by dreaming. In the wolf dream, then, we have to do with one of those "experiences which occurred in very early childhood and were not understood at the time but which were *subsequently* understood and interpreted" (*SE* XII, 149; his italics). And we can now say that the double arrow sign ' $\rightleftharpoons$ ' represents the double movement of all psychical deferment, which takes place by a bipolar[51] process of remembering (forward arrow) and understanding (rearward arrow). Furthermore, the long formula proposed in the first section of this essay can be seen as having special relevance to the case of the Wolf-man within the setting provided by Piaget. How this is so is indicated in the diagram given below, where I have attempted to correlate the formula with early events in the Wolf-man's life, with stages of understanding (ranging from infantile non-understanding to explicitly conscious understanding in the analytic situation), and with modes of symbolic thought (ranging from a pre-symbolic sensori-motor stage, in which the only signs are perceptual indices, to the expressly verbal signs employed in psychoanalytic therapy). Of course, the diagram itself is a symbolic construct and a highly abbreviated one at that, but it does suggest that what might appear to be utterly contingent and unconnected events in the early history of an individual—an innocuous nap in the parental bedroom, a dream of wolves two and a half years later, an ensuing phobia—may give rise to a more rigorous analysis, an analysis that is not at all incompatible with Piaget's seemingly so different findings: indeed, that serves to bear them out.

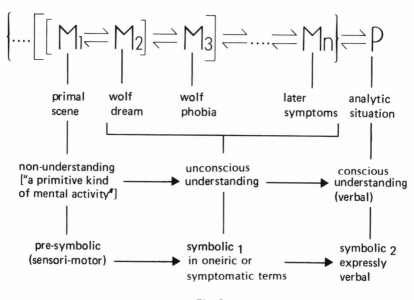

$$\left\{\cdots\left[\left[M_1 \rightleftharpoons M_2\right] \rightleftharpoons M_3\right] \rightleftharpoons \cdots \rightleftharpoons M_n\right\} \rightleftharpoons P$$

| primal scene | wolf dream | wolf phobia | later symptoms | analytic situation |

non-understanding ["a primitive kind of mental activity"] ⟶ unconscious understanding ⟶ conscious understanding (verbal)

pre-symbolic (sensori-motor) ⟶ symbolic 1 in oneiric or symptomatic terms ⟶ symbolic 2 expressly verbal

Fig. 8

Part IV

Let us attempt to draw things together. We began with the mystery of deferred action by memory as this was recognized by Freud in the case history of the Wolf-man. Deferred action was seen to imply — in fact, to require — a deferred understanding that occurs by an "advance in intellectual development" which Freud failed to pinpoint. In perplexity at this impasse, we turned to Piaget's research on memory in childhood, research which indicates that memory *evolves* and does so systematically, in accordance with the evolution of intelligence. And if intelligence evolves so too does understanding, for intelligence is defined by Piaget precisely as "the faculty of understanding and invention."[52] Understanding, then, can operate in a deferred fashion — indeed, in a certain sense, it always must — because it advances by "gradual organizations closely dependent on the structuring activities of intelligence" (MI, 380). But this is of course also descriptive of *memory*, even if memory has the added characteristic of being concerned exclusively with the past — whereas understanding can range over the present and even over certain parts of the future.

The primary point is not just that memory and understanding are parallel processes but that they *overlap* or *coincide* in crucial measure. We cannot remember without, to some extent and however unconsciously (witness the wolf dream), understanding what we remember, just as we cannot understand anything at all (including the future) without drawing upon memory. Piaget helps us to grasp how this coincidence, this *Deckung,* is possible: it is possible precisely because of schemes which, borrowed from intelligence, are common to understanding and remembering alike. Schemes represent the third terms — Kant called them "third things," "mediating representations"[53] — that tie together memory and intelligence, and thus memory and understanding. And if this is so:

> it is no longer possible to distinguish between intelligence as the faculty of understanding and invention and memory as the faculty of conservation and retention. For memory, as the organization of the past, makes use of the pre-operational and operational schemes [belonging to] intelligence.[54]

These schemes organize memory and in so doing make it into more than an image or picture of the past; they make it into an *understanding remembering* it.

The main lines of the mystery have been illuminated. Deferred action by memory occurs because memory itself is developmental and possesses a cognitive component, understanding, that is at one with intelligence, the source of the schematizing activity of mind. No wonder that the Wolf-man's first (and still unconscious) comprehension of the primal scene was deferred for two and a half years! No wonder, either, that it took at least twenty years more to bring this understanding (if not the memory itself) to conscious awareness and then only in analysis with Freud! Yet all significant remembering, I would venture, requires just such a gradual and drawn-out deferment if it is to reach the depths of understanding at which depth psychology aims—and perhaps philosophy too. Plato, after all, considered philosophy a process of very gradually regained recollection: a lifelong *anamnesis* of Forms requiring the infinite patience and the prolongation of the midwife's art of *maieusis*. (It was also Plato who said that "understanding and discourse are the same thing" [*Sophist* 263e]—anticipating Freud's conviction that unless the content of memories is put into words they will not be liberated or liberating: psychoanalysis "brings to an end the operative force of the [traumatic experience] which was not abreacted in in the first instance, by allowing its strangulated affect to find a way out through speech."[55] Thus the Wolf-man's final understanding of his chaotic infancy occurred in the discourse he held, the talking he did, with Freud in analysis.)

But if the mystery has been clarified, a problem remains, and it is in addressing myself to this that I shall draw to a close. The schemes operative in understanding are for Piaget ineluctably cognitive; they stem from intelligence alone. And yet we would not want to say that the Wolf-man at age four had only come to a better intellectual grasp of the primal scene he witnessed when eighteen months old. Although this is certainly an integral part of his belated understanding—various causal schemes, such as those discussed in Part III of *Memory and Intelligence,* are surely involved in his deferred understanding of this scene—he understood something else besides. This "something else" cannot be accounted for by cognitive schemes—or even by the "affective schemes" postulated by Piaget to explain unconscious activities of various sorts.[56] For a *distinctly different* kind of schematism was also at work in "the chaos of the [Wolf-man's] unconscious"—as it no doubt still is in ours, for each of us is much more like the Wolf-man than most of us would care to admit. This different schematism is that of *psychosexuality,* to use Freud's revealingly ambiguous term for that whole region of our mind and behavior reductively called "sexual" in everyday parlance. It is startling to realize that Freud describes psychosexuality in terms almost identical to those which Piaget employs to delineate the development of intelligence. First, psychosexuality evolves in *stages* and even in three primary ones — oral, anal and genital — as if to echo Piaget's sensori-motor, representational and operational stages. Second, psychosexuality results in the *organization* of libido, and when Freud speaks of "pre-genital organization" as a technical term, one cannot help being reminded of Piaget's pre-operational modes of cognitive organization. Third, psychosexuality develops "spontaneously,"[57] a term which Piaget uses as well to characterize the emergence of cognitive schemes.

Without searching for further parallels, and wary of the perils of parallels of this sort,[58] I want only to suggest that more than one type of "transformative organization" is at work in the formation of childhood memories. At least *two* basic kinds of schemes "intervene in the very organization of memory considered as a form of retention" (*MI*, 383): cognitive *and* psychosexual. The fact that the first stem from intelligence and the second from instinct should not trouble us, and all the less so if the instinct in question is called Eros, the animator and moving force of the very knowledge sought by intelligence. Whatever their ultimate provenance (and Piaget is as vague in defining his overall conception of intelligence as Freud is in defining instincts, which are said to be "mythical entities, magnificent in their indefiniteness" [*SE* XXII, 95]), both cognitive and psychosexual schemes are indispensable to memory and to the work of memory, i.e., the recapture of the past in the new understanding of the present. What Piaget says of pre-operational and operational schemes may be regarded as true of pre-genital and genital schemes as well: "the individual continuously reorganizes the past in his schemes" (*MI*, 381).

Thus we might say in conclusion that unless the scheme of genitality (or, still more specifically, of negative Oedipality) was in operation on Christmas eve, 1890,[59] in a child asleep on an enormous estate on the banks of the Dneiper River in deepest Russia, the wolf dream would not have occurred that fateful winter night — nor therefore the wolf phobia and the successor symptoms that brought the Wolf-man to Vienna in 1910 to seek Freud's help. Nor therefore "From the History of an Infantile Neurosis," the official title of Freud's greatest case history. Nor therefore psychoanalysis as we know it.[60] Nor therefore any way of supplementing Piaget's account of memory with one that points to different, and perhaps equally important, modes of organizing and schematizing childhood memories — and thus also of understanding understanding in childhood and adulthood more adequately. For if "the child's memory reflects his level of understanding," and if understanding is conceived as "the manner in which [the child] structures the experiences he has registered in terms of a code that varies with the schemes available to him" (*MI*, 210), then memory and understanding are themselves functions of psychosexuality as well as of intelligence. Just as we have seen that memory and understanding belong together indissolubly, so intelligence and psychosexuality are indissoluble sources of the diverse schemes by which in remembering the figurative becomes operative, the image a sign, the mark a meaning, the trace a testament. And so too can we say, at least, that Piaget and Freud belong together as themselves indissociable sources of our understanding of what remembering is all about.

References

1 Jean Piaget, *Play, Dreams, and Imitation in Childhood,* trans. C. Gattegno and F. H. Hodgson (New York: Norton, 1962), p. 182. (Hereafter cited as '*PDI*'.)

2 These volumes, translated by James Strachey and published by Hogarth Press (London, 1953-74), will hereafter be referred to as '*SE.*'

3 Nevertheless, Piaget makes an exception of himself by recognizing the importance of a screen memory from his own childhood. Cf. *PDI*, 187-188n.

4 Jean Piaget, *Memory and Intelligence,* trans. A. J. Pomerans (New York: Basic Books, 1973), pp. 18-19. Note also p. 131: "all our [adult] memories, no matter how trivial, isolable, or individualized, involve a host of spatial, temporal, causal, and other relations, and a whole hierarchy of planes of reality . . . so much so that they cannot be divorced from a schematism too complex to be grasped by the subject's consciousness." (*Memory and Intelligence* will hereafter be referred to as '*MI.*')

5. "A system of affective schemas is comparable to a system of intellectual schemes, if it is [indeed] true that they are complementary aspects of a single total reality, the system of schemes of real or virtual action" (*PDI*, 210).

6 On this point, see Ernest Schachtel, "On Memory and Childhood Amnesia," in *Metamorphosis* (New York: Basic Books, 1959), pp. 279-322.

7 "The most general result of our investigations has been to reveal the importance of mnemonic schematizations *at any age* and to show that they evolve as a function of the development of intelligence" (*MI*, 381; my italics). "The study of children's memory gives us insight into qualitatively distinct stages that illuminate the very organization of [adult] memory" (*MI*, 19).

8 "Even when everything is finished and the patients have been overborne by the force of logic and have been convinced by the therapeutic effect accompanying the emergence of precisely these [reconstructions] — when, I say, the patients themselves accept the fact that they thought this or that, they often add: 'But I can't *remember* having [experienced] it.' " (*SE* II, p. 300; Freud's italics)

9 *SE* III, 154; Freud italicizes the second sentence. Cf. also *ibid.*, p. 164: "it is not the experiences themselves which act traumatically but their revival as *a memory*" (his italics).

10 Aristotle, *De Memoria et Reminiscentia*, trans. R. Sorabji in his *Aristotle on Memory* (Providence: Brown University Press, 1972), p. 47 (449 a 15).

11 *Ibid.*, p. 52 (451 a 15-16).

12 *SE* XVII, 109; SE I, 365-7.

13 It will hardly do to credit special "sexual researches," as Freud does at SE XVII, 57-8;, for they too draw on the understanding in question.

14   He does so elsewhere as well, for example, in *On The Development of Memory and Identity*, trans. E. Duckworth (Barre, Mass.: Clark University Press, 1968), p. 5: "a memory-image is not simply the prolongation of the perception of the model [to be remembered]. On the contrary, it seems to act in a symbolic manner so as to reflect the subject's assimilation "schèmes," that is, the way in which he *understood* the model (I say "understood" and not "copied," which is an entirely different thing)" (his italics).

15 On this point, see *MI*, 115 and 205.

16 Kant, *Critique of Pure Reason*, trans. N. K. Smith (New York: Humanities Press, 1950), p. 182.

17 *Ibid.*

18 On this point, see *MI*, 392.

19 For the full picture, see *MI*, 392-5. On p. 377, Piaget says that "the reconstructive memory evolves with age, just as do recall and recognition."

20 The memory-image is a symbol of "the assimilations to the schemes which [the child] has made in the presence of the model" (*MI*, 95). The scene is assimilated as a potential result of his own actions or operations, and these latter are specified schematically.

21 *MI*, 70: see also 87, 92 and 396. In what follows, I shall not distinguish between "operative" and "operational" in any rigorous way.

22 *MI*, 397. See also 404 and, indeed, all of 395-409.

23 The full statement is: "the conservation of schemes and of memories can only co-exist by virtue of their mutual dependence, generally to the advantage of both systems, however different they may be, or precisely because they are so different" (*MI*, 397). The whole question of the conservation of schemes vs. the conservation of "memory in the strict sense" (i.e., recognition, reconstruction, recall) is taken up in the Introduction and resolved only toward the end of the General Conclusion.

24 "While the schematism of intelligence tends toward the extra-temporal . . . the function of memory in the strict sense is . . . the comprehension of the past by the representation and temporal localization of events or objects belonging to that past as such" (*MI*, 397). The past as such is "limited and frozen" (399) and thus can be represented only by figuration: "When it comes to knowledge of the past or re-membrance, the figurative elements can no longer be deployed at will (as in the case of the present or future) because past reality can only be what it once was: whence the fundamental, and in this case the privileged, role of figurative factors in what we have called memory in the strict sense" (404).

25 For this claim, see *MI*, 379 and 395.

26 'III' signifies success by trial and error while 'IV' involves a systematic solution of the problem. See MI, 29-30.

27 Concerning this point, see *MI*, 45-6.

28 *MI*, 46. The scheme has evolved because of its activation and exercise in the child's ongoing activities and because it seeks equilibration by a kind of inner *nisus:* see p. 46 and esp. p. 60: "the close link between the mnemonic level and that of the operational schemes demonstrates that it is the spontaneous equilibration of the lat-ter, combined with further practice and the demand for inner coherence, which governs the organization of memory and which, in the particular case of seriations, explains the exceptional advances we encountered."

29 The regressions occur in the periods between 1 hour and one week, and between one week and six months. See *MI*, 76-83.

30 In contrast, younger subjects of 4 to 5 years remember the continuous figure poorly too, which suggests that its lack of figurative support is more crucial at this earlier point. See *MI*, 91-2.

31 *MI*, 95. Cf. also p. 341: "what the child remembered was not the figure he had perceived as such, but a modification of it in accordance with his operational schemes." On the same point, see also p. 383.

32 For a discussion of these results, see *MI*, 147-51.

33 See Table 14 on *MI*, 153, for the exact results.

34 See *MI*, ch. 13, esp. 234-7, on the incomprehensible causal process.

35 *MI*, 167; the treatment of this figure is found at 165-71.

36 Indeed, the force of understanding is such that in this case perception may even be said to be *corrected* by it: cf. *MI*, 171.

37 On this point, see MI, 26 (*"the code itself is susceptible to change* during the construction of operational schemes") and p. 263: "progress and regress do not depend simply on the encoding and decoding process—the code itself seems to improve with the formation of operational structures." See also pp. 192 and 200, and the claim in *On The Development of Memory and Identity* that "the final memory, then, is indeed a decoding, but it is the decoding of a code which has changed, which is better structured than it was before" (p. 5).

38 For a more complete discussion, see *MI*, 386-7.

39 Another way of putting this is to say that "If the memory does indeed show signs of becoming more efficient at encoding and decoding data as the child matures, the code itself remains unchanged." (*MI*, 379).

40 See Henri Bergson, *Matter and Memory,* trans. N. M. Paul and W. S. Palmer (New York: Anchor, 1959), pp. 22-3, 119-23, 173-4.

41 Cf. Freud's remarks to this effect in "Repeating, Remembering and Working-through," *SE* XII, 148-9.

42 *MI*, 126. The reference in Freud is to Letter 52 to Fliess (6 December, 1896).

43 Piaget adds by way of clarification: "except that for him the present was less strongly influenced by memory as a form of representation than by the overall schemes of interpersonal behavior . . . acquired in contact with one's closest relatives" (*MI*, 381).

44 Piaget explicitly links imagery, dreams, and memory at *MI*, 378.

45 Memory is "intelligence *qua* knowledge of the past" (*MI*, 378).

46 "Every type of mnemonic recall involves an image" (*MI*, 395); but elsewhere there is an admission of recall by words alone: for example, p. 380.

47 On this distinction, see esp. *MI*, 382: the *scheme* is "an instrument of generalization," while a *schéma* is an abbreviation or simplification of a perception or a memory: "a law governing the (mental or graphic) image as such."

48 "All figurative memories are based on more or less differentiated schemes" (*MI*, 405). Cf. the whole discussion on 404-5.

49 The scene with Grusha at two and a half years old is a deferred imitation by *external* action of the Wolf-man's father's role in the primal scene. It is of interest that it occurs *before* the wolf dream. See *SE* XVII, 90-96, 107-8.

50 Freud specifically calls the wolf dream a form of "deferred action" at *SE* XVII, 45n, 47, 109; it is said to involve "deferred understanding" at *ibid.*, 37n, 58, 77.

51 The term is Piaget's. See *MI*, 403: bipolarity "is not the same thing [as dualism] because it implies an inseparable link instead of a plurality of factors."

52 *MI*, 380. Intelligence is also defined at *MI* 390, as "the higher equilibrated form of cognitive functions" — among which is memory.

53 Kant, *Critique of Pure Reason*, p. 181.

54 *MI*, 380. The passage continues: "though in a quite specific way, namely, in the construction, conservation, and reconstruction of the concrete images of particular events, judged to have occurred in reality."

55 *SE* II, 17; in italics. Cf. also *ibid.*, p. 6.

56 Note that Piaget defines affective schemes in *Memory and Intelligence* as "schemes of interpersonal behavior" (p. 381). A full discussion of affective schemes is found at *PDI*, 188-93, 204-11.

57 Freud's use of this term occurs at *SE* VII, 191: "spontaneously from internal causes."

58 One important difference, for example, is that regression is a much more common — and momentous — feature among psychosexual schemes: as is attested to by the whole period of latency. On the *lack* of regression to pre-operational levels, see *MI*, 24.

59 By the Julian calendar; 1891 by the Gregorian calendar, in which the Wolf-man's day of birth would be January 6, 1887 and not December 24, 1886.

60 Note that it was precisely the analysis of the Wolf-man that led Freud to complete his theory of the stages of psychosexual organization. (See Strachery's comment on this in *SE* XVII, 5-6, 126.)

Discussion

Marvin Levine: Is Piaget's theory of memory in fact the Aristotelian theory of memory? Piaget says that you get parallel results when you demonstrate that the child simply copies pictures. That would imply that the child could very well have a mental picture, a simple photographic reproduction of what was shown, but he has difficulty in copying that picture. Memory itself is photographic. The common problem to both perceptual and memorial phenomena is in the output.

Edward S. Casey: Why do you want to posit this photographic model?

Levine: I don't want to posit it. I'm suggesting that the data are consistent with that interpretation.

Hans Furth: Not really. Memory changes. You would still have to explain how this copy picture changes.

Levine: Are you inferring that the memory changes from the data?

Furth: Of course.

Levine: But did you get the same data from pictures? Do you get the same changes for the same data?

Furth: But you can only confirm them if you have their memory extended. If you ask them six months later, and if you find the memory has changed, it shows that something active is going on.

Casey: Yes. Something active is going on, but he is asking whether this internal image which was in itself and by itself purely reproductive is changed? Of course, we can never know. There may well be such a thing, but what Professor Furth is saying is that any actual effort to describe what that image is, or for the child to draw it, shows it to be non-reproductive.

Levine: I know, but even copying directly turns out to be non-reproductive.

Casey: Yes. That seems like a problem.

Furth: But that is not a problem, because copying is always like that. Copying is based upon the child's understanding. Perception is based upon understanding. And memory is based upon understanding.

Levine: I say it is a parallel. It is not a problem. If you posit that the memory-image changes somehow, it will accord better with the reality of the child.

Furth: I do not say that the memory-image changes.

Casey: It is the scheme that changes.

Furth: The scheme changes to construct what we call the memory-image. The whole point is that there is no such thing as a memory-image. What we have is an understanding and what changes is the understanding.

Levine: I insist that for Piaget the child really has a picture. We cannot even see it, but the child keeps *it* for a while. He will give us the same results. Six months later when he peeks at the picture, he gives you imperfect or somewhat perfect results . . .

Casey: Of course, but I don't think it really contravenes the most important point that Piaget is trying to make, which is that the initial perception, as well as the early memory and even memory an hour later, is distorted because the operative scheme is not adequate to the perception and therefore to the memory of the object. So for Piaget, it does not produce a problem. I am still not clear on why it is a problem for you.

Levine: I am saying that it is an alternative interpretation—an Aristotelian interpretation. For the child, who is too young to reproduce appropriately whether from a picture or from memory, we have to gauge from what was presented to him. That's all. When you ask him six months later, he draws out that picture.

Casey: If anything, that seems to be in conflict with the notion that he must not have such an image if his very perception is not itself adequate.

Levine: No. The perception is fine. He simply cannot draw it. He cannot give you the output.

Casey: Okay. But then you are driven to a kind of dualism of perception and activity which seems to me to be problematic in itself—although not impossible.

Levine: But that must exist. We have the initial confrontation in which we present him with a picture and he cannot draw it appropriately. He assimilates it to his schemes as it exists. This implies that an Aristotelian interpretation of the memory is possibly correct.

Casey: Yes. But I think that it is unnecessary baggage. I do not know why you would want to endorse his notion of an absolutely perfect image which then is misinterpreted, modified and misremembered until finally mishandled. Indeed, the picture itself is mishandled.

Roger Schvaneveldt: It seems that your account of Freud's reinterpretation of earlier memories presupposes the notion of a copy memory as well. Otherwise what is there to be reinterpreted? The only alternative I see is that what the child remembers is the scheme and that the scheme has undergone change. The child, in fact, needs the scheme he was using earlier for other experiences. The child does need a scheme for dealing with the set of unseriated rods. If the scheme for unseriated rods undergoes development every time, the child would no longer be able to deal adequately with unseriated rods. What I am saying is that you cannot put memory solely in schemata and still have a reinterpretation of a learning experience.

Casey: It is not put solely in terms of schemes. As Piaget states, there is always a figurative component. The scheme is never sufficient. It is always a partial and never a complete reproduction.

Furth: Did the Wolf-man scene ever actually take place?

Casey: We don't know.

Furth: See. It is quite irrelevant. It may have been pure projection on the part of the child. What does Freud say?

Casey: Freud, as you may remember, vacillates back and forth. It doesn't worry Freud because it could have been another experience. Indeed Freud says at one point, it could have been a scene of sheep copulating with each other on an enormous estate near the river Dnieper in Russia which the Wolf-man projected upon his own parents. It doesn't matter that much exactly what it starts from. What is important is where it ends. That is the way in which he rejoins Piaget. What is crucial about the memory of the wolf dream, whatever its exact origin, is its function, content, and structure on the night when he dreamt it.

Schvaneveldt: It makes a great difference whether you call it memory or fantasy.

Casey: No. It has to be based on some figurative, genuine, and perceptual content. It may be misidentified and incorrectly labelled by the Wolf-man himself at that earlier point. Perhaps he was confused. It is certainly possible. He may have misinterpreted any number of things. It could have been his parents merely lying in bed, which he imagined in such a vivid fashion that he thought he saw . . . . Of course, there are memories of fantasies as much as memories of perceptions. There is no reason why, even if the original event were entirely a matter of fantasy, it too could not become the nucleus.

Schvaneveldt: Then memory becomes irrelevant or unimportant in a sense?

Casey: Not for Freud. He would say that it could become extremely important depending upon the moment of its revival. If it revives itself at a critical moment, then it is important. If not, it's indifferent. That fits in fairly well with Piaget, because even if the original experience were wholly imagined, memory-images, for Piaget, may return in force. They can take the place of perception. Part of the adequacy or, at least, the scope of his theory is to avoid, as Freud does, forcing us to choose between a genuine perception and genuine imagination.

Question₁: The problem with that, though, is that the original perception or image is wholly imagined. Its figurative components could not be beyond the schemes of which the child is capable at that time. Where then is the figurative component which is later reinterpreted beyond those schemes? There is no information if it is beyond the schemes. When reinterpreted later, what is reinterpreted?

Furth: The child has a traumatic dream when he was 4 years old. Obviously the trauma relates to *something* the child had experienced in the past. That is where the memory component comes in. Whether it is the specific thing is largely irrelevant because, for the child's psychological life, it is a memory. Something has happened to the child.

Question₁: But an experience only within the scheme that is available to the child at that time.

Furth: Why do you stress that? I mean that's obviously true.

Question₁: Because if we reinterpret, there must be some information there beyond the scheme which the child can later be able to understand.

Furth: Why does it have to be beyond the scheme? I don't understand this.

Charles Scott: Therapeutically, it makes no difference whether the event occurred or not. It is the presence of the memory or the image that counts. Interpretively, *vis-à-vis* an understanding of mind, it makes an enormous difference, because there is a claim about the reality of memory which is basically not a claim in the interests of therapy. When you make a claim about memory, you are saying that either memory is the restructuring of images or memory is direct access to a non-imaginal event which I found ambivalent in Freud and in your remarks on Freud. It makes all the difference in the world on which side you go. You are right. It is a question of whether, interpretively speaking, we are dealing with restructured images or with an event common to the various restructurings. It is that issue of what is common to the restructuring that has been raised at several places. You have tended to respond in terms of what makes sense for therapy.

Casey: True. That was Freud's main concern. But I also think that you are on to something here. You are asking about that extra unassimilated component in the experience. Could it be present as an image? I am not sure that there is any reason why it could not be. One could have an imaginative experience which nevertheless one was not capable of comprehending at the time, but whose significance could be fathomed only much later.

Schvaneveldt: But that would place you within the scope of copy theory.

Casey: Well, I don't think it is copy theory in Aristotle's sense, in which you had to copy the whole object in its totality. That's strict copy theory.

Susan Bordo: But in order to reach that stage once he had developed the schemata, doesn't the child have to make reference to that copy at the original moment?

Casey: I don't think so.

Susan Buck-Morss: How else can he approximate it then?

Casey: He now understands the shape and structure of these components, which, until then, were amorphous, imperfectly shaped, and not fully assimilated. Now he is able, by means of this increasingly available scheme of seriation, to put those components in order. It is a matter of disordered data which is reordered and better ordered.

Scott: Is that data included in an imaginal scheme?

Casey: That's an important question.

Scott: That's what we are worrying about. In other words, is it data that is organized and then reorganized? Or is it data that is left out of the organization, but later incorporated into the organization?

Casey: Both possibilities could obtain and do obtain in perception.

Scott: If you had an image of intercourse, and that image continues. then at this level it means violent activity. At this level, it means mother and father experiencing sex. Then you have the copy theory as the foundation for the continuity of symbolic schemes. But the issue is the translation from scheme to scheme in both Piaget and Freud.

Casey: In a way, Freud does acknowledge this, because he searches frantically for indices of the real scene. Perhaps he really does suspect that such an index would help his explanation a great deal. It would avoid the problem that you rightly raise. It is very hard to see where in the world this unassimilated content comes from in imagination. Actually, though, I really think that there is such. We do have imaginative experiences which we do not fully assimilate or fully comprehend at the time. We think about them later. We suddenly realize: "That was an image of my Uncle Joe that I had a week ago." This could just be personal idiosyncrasy, but I think that it is at least possible. That is all I would claim. If it is possible, then it is possible to have an early imaginative experience whose components are not identified. The information is left radically unspecified, but still, with increasing development, we could better specify it.

Furth: If you think of sensori-motor learning, you have exactly the same problem. A two-month-old baby learns some figurative contingency. How is it stored in the baby? Would we say that the baby has a concept of an image? That is *our* way of talking about it. It is part of the baby's organization. Suppose the baby knows that this door leads into the kitchen and that the other door leads into the bathroom. How is this stored in the baby — or the dog, for that matter? It is exactly the same problem. That is why it is easy to say that the organism — the person — has an image. We call it a learned image. But isn't a learned image a memory-image? It is part of the child's behavior. The child knows this door. We call it recognition. What is the basis of recognition?

Casey: Even *that* is unassimilated content. But something is there. That is your point.

Furth: We cannot do away with the memory trace. It must be there. Otherwise it isn't memory. The memory base is the material base, I would say. What counts is what the person does with the trace or result. Memory is never just memory.

Casey: Although what is a memory? That still remains the mystery — at least insofar as it is taken to be a pure copy.

PIAGET, ADORNO, AND THE POSSIBILITIES OF DIALETICAL OPERATIONS*

Susan Buck-Morss

> The kind of happiness that could awaken envy in us exists only in the air we have breathed, among human beings with whom we might have spoken, among women who might have given themselves to us. With other words, in the image of happiness there whirls, inalienably, the image of redemption. It is the same with the image of the past, which is the concern of history. The past carries with it a secret index by means of which it refers to redemption. Are we not ourselves, then, stroked by a breath of the air which touched those before us? Does there not exist in voices to which we lend our ear an echo of those now silenced? Have not the women whom we woo had sisters of whom they no longer have knowledge? If it is so, then there exists a secret conspiracy between past generations and our own. Then we have been awaited on the earth. Then there is granted to us, as to every generation which came before us, a *weak* messianic power, to which the past has claim. This claim cannot be dismissed cheaply. The historical materialist knows that. — Walter Benjamin[1]

Cogency and play are the two poles of philosophy. — Theodor W. Adorno[2]

Several years ago I wrote an article[3] which brought together two previously separate areas of discourse, Piaget's theory of cognitive development and Adorno's philosophy of negative dialectics. The essay was an attempt to account for the fact that in the cross-cultural application of Piaget tests, non-Western children score significantly lower than their Western peers, implying that the cognitive development of the former, particularly in Third-World countries, is somehow "retarded."[4]

The gist of my argument was this: Piaget chose to examine the development of formal operations because he wanted to establish a psychology
which was universal, hence "scientific," according to his definition, and he
made the assumption that formal structures of thought were universal
precisely because they were abstract, while particular content, which could
be separated from form, was inessential, contingent on cultural and environmental factors. But according to Adorno (who was following the early
work of Georg Lukács),[5] this separation of form from content, far from
universal, was itself the product of history: the abstract form of cognition
which the present era accepted as second nature, while appearing to be
divorced from the social world, was in fact its mirror image. Specifically,
the abstract formalism which Piaget focussed upon in thought emerged
historically in urban, commercial cultures, and became the dominant
logical structure when, with the rise of Western industrial capitalism, it
became the dominant social structure. With the advent of wage labor, production as well as exchange acquired abstract value, and the purely formal
language of mathematics (the language of commercial transactions)
became the expression of the social relations of production as well as those
of the marketplace. It is thus not surprising that in Third-world countries,
especially in rural areas where social structures of kinship have not yet been
pre-empted by those of market exchange, children do not develop their
capacities for abstract, formal cognition, and in testing for this, the
development of other cognitive modes may have gone unnoticed.

Piaget indeed recognizes that the child's cognitive development does not
occur in a vacuum, but depends on his or her acting upon objects. But
those objects are simply given, the furniture of the child's environment,
which provide the occasion for cognitive development but do not determine it substantively.[6] Even at the level of concrete operations, where some
of his most interesting work has been done, Piaget assumes that the most
significant factor is not so much what the child can do in this concrete
world, but how quickly he can do without it. It is the form, not the arbitrary contents of the classification and conservation tests, that is important. They test for the ability to identify an abstract quality that remains constant despite change in the object's appearance and despite the
fact that human beings have acted upon it; and this directly parallels the
ability to conceptualize commodities and labor in mathematical terms of
abstract exchange.

To summarize: built into Piaget's theory is an epistemological mistake.
A socio-economic bias impairs his vision and prevents him from seeing
that, at the level of formal operations, thought has far from left the mun-

dane world behind, but only incorporated it more deeply, at a social structural level, rather than merely a perceptual, empirical one — as, indeed,
has Piaget himself. For he is no more divorced from interaction with the
objective world than are the children in his experiments. The truth of his
theory emerges precisely when, from the point of view of his own "scientific" intentions, it failed, that is, not by establishing a universal
psychology, but by accurately, if unintentionally, reflecting the structure
of his own society for which, then, his tests are a very good indication of
how well a child can function cognitively.

This argument provides a dialectical exercise, an applied illustration of
Adorno's critical method.[7] Its aim is not merely to demonstrate that
superstructure and substructure, consciousness and social reality, are
dialectically interrelated, but to provide an intellectual experience which,
in contrast to Piaget's tests for reversible operations already achieved, in-
vites a new level of insight, one which is in fact *irreversible*. For if the argument has made its point, it puts the texts of Piagetian literature in a new
context so that they can never be read in quite the same way again.

We can put this to the test with an example. The Harvard psychologist
Kohlberg has developed a theory of moral development paralleling
Piaget's theory of cognitive development. Kohlberg assumes that abstract
mental processes are by definition universal, free of particular social content, and defines moral maturity as the ability to divorce morality from
content and to think in accord with formal moral principles. In a seminal
article providing an introduction to his theory, he reports on a series of experiments to illustrate the development of abstract comprehension
generally:

> (1) *Preconceptual* (age 3-4 years). Money is not recognized as a symbol
> of value different from other objects and it is not understood that money
> is exchanged in purchase and sale transactions . . . .
>
> (2) *Intermediate* (age 4-5 years). Children recognize that money
> transfer is required in stores, but do not recognize that the transfer is an
> exchange of equal economic value. The exchange of work as job for salary
> is not understood, nor is the scarcity of money understood . . . .
>
> (3) *Concrete operational* (age 6-8 years). Children recognize money
> transactions as involving a logical relation of reversible, reciprocal, and
> equal exchange values. They understand that the storekeeper must pay
> money to others for his goods, they understand the work-salary exchange,
> and the scarcity or "conservation" of money.[3]

Here the tables are turned on the tester, for the empirical research Kohlberg cites in fact documents that the child is learning not abstract thinking but concrete economics: these are the developmental stages in being introduced to the riddle of commodities. Without knowing it, and precisely against his intent, Kohlberg's text allows an immanent criticism of his formalist position, and in the process provides evidence for our own.

Decentering, Dialectics and Equilibration

The immanent critical procedure of allowing a text to bear witness against itself was characteristic of Adorno. I am tempted to call it a process of "decentering," although he himself did not, and although the word, now the pet term of a wide variety of structuralists including Piaget, has lost precision of meaning. But perhaps the very ambivalence of the term helps to clarify the difference between Adorno and Piaget.

In Piaget's theory, "decentering" refers to the moment at each stage of cognitive development when, in order to reconcile disparities between conceptual schema and empirical experience, an egocentric cognitive position is relinquished in favor of a more "objective" one.[9] This process is complete by adolescence, when the child's space has become universal space, the child's time historical time, and earlier illusions of omnipotence have been replaced by comprehension of external laws of causation.

Significantly, Piaget concentrates on just those formal categories of time, space and causality which the bourgeois philosopher Kant maintained were the *a prioris* of rational experience.[10] But for Adorno, Kant's Copernican revolution in philosophy implied another kind of egocentrism. It assumed as the structure of experience an identity between the rational subject and the empirical objects which it reasoned about. Adorno described his own philosophy as giving Kant's "Copernican revolution an axial turn" toward *non*-identity,[11] by exploding all attempts of the rational subject to find itself in the world which, claimed Adorno, was decidedly not rational. As a materialist, Adorno insisted on the priority of the external world which — this implied another kind of decentering — imposed its structure (the formal, reified structure of commodity production) on consciousness,[12] and which it was the task of reason to think against rather than adapt itself to.

In contrast, and in complicity with his own definition of "decentering," Piaget's theory of "equilibration" holds that cognitive structures generate higher, more stable (albeit not static) forms when faced with contradictions which its existing forms cannot resolve, or, to use his biological metaphor, when it is subject to stimuli from without for which it cannot compensate.[13] It has been suggested that this conception is a dialectical one.[14] If this is so, then only at the most simplistic, *un*dialectical level — we might refer to it as Stage 1 of dialectical thinking — which is found in the crude schematization of Hegelianism into the catchwords: thesis, antithesis, synthesis; or, in the automatic evolutionism of Engels' *Dialectics of Nature* which was known in Adorno's time as "vulgar Marxism."[15] The limitation of this conception of dialectics is that it posits a dialectical interrelationship between subject and object (in this case, between the child and his environment) while at the same time thinking it can bracket out the observer, as if the theorist were not himself a part of the dialectical process he was describing. As Adorno and his theoretical colleagues have argued, this attempt to describe dialectics from the outside either leads into the static dead-end of metaphysics,[16] or posits an automatic progress via dialectical evolution that from the perspective of the twentieth century appears indefensibly optimistic.[17]

Adorno was fully aware of his own socio-historical relativity. His theory intervenes actively in promoting historical change because it doesn't just describe a dialectical operation, it *is* one — at Stage 3 at least, and he takes us there with him. What Piaget views positively as a natural tendency of the mind to seek stable states through assimilating and accommodating the outside world in its given form, Adorno (setting that whole world in question) views negatively, as a lamentable social condition. For him it is the tendency, nourished by the mindless culture of mass society, for the mind to conform to the given state of things, and it represents a retardation rather than an advance: reason, faced with real contradictions, mistakes them for logical contradictions, and spends its energies trying to eliminate the latter rather than the former. If this tendency appears natural, Adorno would argue, then this is because social reality has become "second nature," accepted unquestionably, which means that consciousness needs to struggle against it all the more strongly.

In fact, it would be accurate to define Adorno's goal as achieving cognitive instability, a *dis*equilibrium between structures of consciousness and those of reality. This is really the heart of his philosophy of "negative dialectics." It sets off a disequilibrium in thinking by stressing nonidentity, and it does this in two ways. First, it takes advantage of the ambivalence between word and thing, arguing, for example, that second nature isn't very natural, since it is the historical product of a particular social structure. But the social structure isn't very social either, because of the alienation and isolation of its members. Such a critical procedure throws thought patterns into disequilibrium by pointing out the difference in identity, that is, the assumed identity between word and thing.[18] Secondly, the process can be reversed, pointing out the identity in difference, showing how two seemingly opposed phenomena have in fact identical structures, as in our initial argument that the structure of abstract formal cognition reflects the social structure of commodity exchange.

It must be made clear that Adorno's procedure in no way implies reductionism. When he analyzes a psychological theory, he indeed translates it into terms of social reality; but when he analyzes a social phenomenon, his focus shifts to the psychological structures which sustain it.[19] There is no hierarchy to the translations from one mode to another but only a shifting of centers.[20] The result is a totally altered conception of causality. For Adorno there is no unequivocal historical "source"[21] of the present, but only a creative, continually renewed discovery of the constellation which the past makes within a constantly changing present. The process is not unlike poetic "troping," whereby an idea undergoes a series of metamorphoses, without any one form being more dominant than the rest.[22]

But Adorno's transformations are not simply variations of a myth. Nor are his negations merely inversions within a system. The function of myths is to provide logical models for overcoming social and cultural contradictions. They thus have the capacity to make coherent and acceptable whatever is self-contradictory in the ideological system: describing origins, they reconstruct the past in order to explain *away* a present anomaly. The function of Adorno's arguments is precisely the opposite. Every one of them, by decentering thought and heightening awareness of contradictions, deconstructs a system, dismantles a myth. Indeed, he made "antisystem" the motto of his philosophy and equated it with a process of "demythification."[23]

Science, Art and Myth

If in Adorno's theory the translation of structures from one modality to another replaces the search for causal origins, this results from the fact that the model for his philosophy was aesthetic experience, not scientific experiment.[24] It is significant that Adorno studied musical composition with Schönberg's disciple Alban Berg: musical meaning emerges in the interruptions of anticipated patterns,[25] rather than, as in experimental science, in the consistencies of results. Moreover, the internal coherence of aesthetic compositions is achieved by articulating the antagonisms between idea and reality rather than reconciling them. As Proust has written, the artwork is constructed out of the "superimposition of two systems," the world of experience and the aesthetic order, and these worlds remain non-identical, in a relation of tension which determines the aesthetic form.[26]

Adorno did not want to make philosophy aesthetic. As he wrote, "most bitterly irreconcilable is that which is similar but which feeds on different centers . . . ."[27] Rather, he refused to see science and art as binary opposites, and instead counterposed knowledge to myth. He defined myth as a closed system, reproducing the ever-identical. In this sense it could be argued that the experimental standardization which has befallen Piaget's tests is far more mythical than art; while knowledge as experience of the unanticipated, the new, possesses that moment of discovery and freedom which was the original impulse of science.[28]

To call Piaget's approach more "scientific" than Adorno's cannot, it seems to me, be substantiated philosophically or empirically. Not only does Piaget's equation of cognitive and biological development amount to the metaphorical translation of psychology into terms of natural science;[29] but it must be conceded that science itself is a metaphor,[30] a belief system in which, as in magic, internal coherence has become a substitute for truth. In *Primitive Classifications,* Durkheim and Mauss note two social functions of belief systems: (1) a speculative function, making intelligible the relation between things; and (2) a moral function, to regulate the conduct of human beings.[31] The scientific belief system which dominates in present-day society seems to have difficulty doing either. Yet the hold of science remains tenacious. As Polanyi has observed, the situation is not unlike that described by Evans-Pritchard among the Zande in Africa who resisted giving up their magical belief systems even when elements in it were demonstrated to be wrong. In our society:

> [a]ny contradiction between a   particular scientific notion and the facts of experience will be explained by other scientific notions . . . . Secured by its circularity and defended further by its epicyclical reserves, science may deny, or at least cast aside as of no scientific interest, whole ranges of experience which to the unscientific mind appear both massive and vital . . . . I conclude that what earlier philosophers have alluded to by speaking of coherence as the criterion of truth is only a criterion of stability. It may equally stabilize an erroneous or a true view of the universe.[32]

The point is, of course, that the "criterion of stability" has crucial political implications. Science is not a neutral language, and the whole no-

tion of value-free knowledge is one of the most insidious myths. By trying
to explain given reality rationally, scientific explanations tend toward the
"equilibration" of social systems, while Adorno's decentering method applies reason against the grain of reality. The important political point is
that power lies not only in the control of the means of production within a
society, but in the *control of the production of meanings* as well.

The Development of Dialectical Operations

Piaget has written: "the principle goal of education is to create men who
are capable of doing new things, not simply repeating what other generations have done," and that its second goal "is to form minds which can be
critical, can verify, and do not accept everything they are offered."[33] Yet
his choice of paradigms, the scientific experiment with its abstract, formal
operations, works unwittingly against this goal because it has no means to
place the "given" itself in question. An education system based on this
model may produce intelligent functionaries — technocrats who, in science,
social analysis, or any other field, apply their rational faculties within existing cognitive and social structures.[34] But it will not encourage the
development of human beings capable of structural innovation.

Piaget insists that "to understand is to invent."[35] But invention turns out
to be no more than a rediscovery of the already dominant mode of
thought, through interaction with an unchanged world. He acknowledges
the importance of "play" in cognitive development. Yet play is not
understood as that creative fantasy of the artist, which in the name of
denied pleasure protests against reality by constructing another world.[36] It
is merely the "predominance of assimilation over accommodation,"[37]
which means that instead of the child submitting to reality, reality is forced
to submit to the child. Play for Piaget is pleasurable only in the sense of
"freedom from conflicts,"[38] of achieving "mastery" over "models of activity" and "acquiring thereby a feeling of virtuosity or power."[39] It is "practice,"[40] "repetition,"[41] and its distinction from serious, "scientific" activities is thus only a matter of degree.[42]

If we are concerned with the capacity not merely to think within existing
cognitive systems and social systems but beyond them, then the constellation of fantasy, criticism and disequilibration which characterizes
Adorno's program might be indeed more relevant for a theory of cognitive
development. What are the possibilities of studying the development of
children's thinking in terms of negative, dialectical operations, based on
principles of non-identity,[43] which, because they shift the cognitive focus

off center, constantly question and challenge not only "reality" but the dominant cognitive schema which purport to describe it adequately?

In the first place, rather than stressing, as does Piaget, the child's ability to synthesize contradictions, we would be interested in just the opposite, the ability to tolerate ambivalence,[44] and moreover, to enjoy its suspense as a moment of creative risk and the potential for new discovery. For example, at the level of perception, in testing for the comprehension of space, we would not assume Piaget's bias for Euclidean geometry or for any formal, measurable system where the synthetic coordination of objects within an unequivocal, universal space is considered the cognitive goal.[45] Instead, we would inquire into the child's ability to play with space so that its meaning is transformed, as in picture games like "spot the object;" or to produce changing patterns out of static representations by shifting the relative depths of spatial planes, as in experiencing a Necker cube.[46] Furthermore, we would not accept Piaget's equation of cognitive maturity with mastery of perspective,[47] a fifteenth-century Florentine invention which reflected the bourgeois cosmology of a man-centered, secular universe. Instead, we would be interested in the child's ability to read deep and complex spatial arrangements, as in a cubist or surrealist painting, or to grasp the paradoxical intellectual spaces in the paintings of Vasarély or the drawings of Escher.[48]

In regard to time, our attention would not be directed at empty, formal time — clock time, which is a measurable constant regardless of what occurs within it, and which functions as "the coordination of motions."[49] Instead, aesthetic experience would again provide a model, in the form of musical rhythm. Maturity would be defined as the ability to grasp increasingly irregular rhythms, moving from the 4/4, repetitive rhythm of a military march to the syncopated rhythms of jazz,[50] to the more sophisticated, asymmetrical rhythms of non-Western music, and the polyrhythmic superimposition of two opposed schemata. An example of the latter (a relatively advanced stage, judging from my own childhood experience) would be those passages in Beethoven's piano sonatas where the left hand plays triplets while the right hand plays couplets; or, rhythmic ambivalence, as in the third movement of the *Eroica* where, to cite Adorno, rhythm "rises up against the existing law until it produces from out of it a new one."[51]

It should be noted that, on the perceptual level of time and space, our approach would represent more a shift in focus than a totally new project.[52] For at least through the stage of concrete operations Piaget's experiments are tied to content, and he is fully aware of the generative power of perceptual ambivalence in accounting for the dynamics of cognitive development. But Piaget views the child as constantly trying to regain perceptual equilibrium; indeed, this is what motivates him to construct new cognitive schemes. In contrast, we are suggesting that, as a form of play akin to artistic creation and as an operation vital to critical thinking, the child may be motivated to abandon perceptual equilibrium, and to construct schemes which aid him in this process.

A more fundamental difference in our approach would be its rejection of Piaget's formal model of mathematics with its stable, reversible operations. Instead, we would turn to language as the expression of cognitive development—not language as a system, but spoken language, with none of the ambivalence of its referents bracketed out.

Piaget's relative lack of concern for language might seem surprising, given the seminal role it plays in the "structuralist" movement with which he identifies. But it is precisely his acknowledged affinity with this group which has led him to make a sharp distinction between language and intelligence. French structuralists deal with language as a system of arbitrary signifiers, the meanings of which are fixed by social convention. As such, they are unconcerned with the generative process of speech, that expressive activity which is central to the linguistic development of the child. On the other hand, the American structuralist Noam Chomsky deals with the generative nature of language, but he does so with a notion of innateness which violates Piaget's most persistent tenet, the *constructive* nature of cognitive development, the fact that its generation is dependent on experience.[53] Piaget has avoided a conflict with fellow structuralists by arguing that since, for example, children combine or dissociate manually before they do it verbally, intelligence "antedates language and is independent of it."[54] Thought comes first and is a spontaneous, individual activity, but language "is a group institution. Its rules are imposed on individuals. One generation coercively transmits it to the next . . . ."[55] Language "profoundly transforms thought," but only in the sense that by submitting to its tyranny, thought "attains its forms of equilibrium by means of a more advanced schematization and a more mobile abstraction."[56] What gets lost in his conception is the constructive moment of speech: to speak is to invent meaning, not only out of the dialectical tension between linguistic convention and the speaker's intention, but out of the gap between signifier and signified which, for Adorno, is the locus of the production of meanings, and the point where play, creativity, and the capacity for critical thinking converge.

In the beginning, the child's language is literal. Objects have priority in the child's world, and every name for them is a proper name. There is no gap between signifier and signified.[57] Adorno's close friend Walter Benjamin, recalling the Old Testament story of Adam as name-giver of God's creatures, called this the language of Paradise before the Fall when, with the babble of human language, words lost their adequacy, because they could not recapture exact and concrete knowledge of the particular.[58] Adorno criticized Benjamin, pointing out the inadequacy of the name: as mimetic reflection, as a simple image of the given, it could not represent anything *but* the given.[59] He acknowledged its utopian promise for the future: the positivism inherent in a language of names would, in fact, be adequate for describing a just society. But for the present, language needed to be critical, using logic to express the illogic of society.

In light of this theoretical speculation, it is perhaps not without significance that when children do begin to use language as a self-contained system of signifiers, they take great pleasure in using the logic of language against the logic of reality. Adherence to grammatical rules can make sense out of nonsense:

> The cow sat on a birch tree
> And nibbled on a pea.[60]

This rhyme is cited by Chukovsky, the Soviet child psychologist, in a book (reissued in Russia sixteen times since its appearance in 1925) which argued strenuously against the position of those socialist realist educators who wanted to eradicate such nonsense in order "to convert every child immediately into a scientist . . . . "[61] Chukovsky notes: "the child thinks of words in pairs, he assumes that every word has a 'twin' — an opposite in meaning or quality."[62] Just so, he continues, sense and nonsense are thought together. Hence, the child's appreciation of nonsense is an indication that he grasps reality: "to be able to respond to these playful rhymes the child must have a knowledge of the real order of things . . . . "[63] Yet at the same time, it is a form of protest, a creative use of language to suggest another reality. Language nonsense which violates the established order of reality, such as the 3 year old's invention: "The birds ring, the bells fly!"[64] is called by Chukovsky the "Topsy-Turvies":

> A most widely used method in these mental games is precisely a reversal
> of the normal relationship of things: ascribing to object A the function of
> object B, and the other way round.[65]

The method described is pure dialectics. Perhaps the child's game of Topsy-Turvies, where humor, knowledge of reality and making believe all find expression, is the ontogenetic origin of negative, dialectical operations.

The gap between signified and signifier, the object and its concept, thus prevents thought from being totally dominated by reality in its given form. However, so Adorno would argue, it also prevents the opposite, the domination of reality by thought. Because human language cannot reinstate the "name," any attempt to absorb the object within the concept, which generalizes through abstraction, has to do violence to the object's uniqueness. Adorno claimed that objects do not go into their concepts without leaving a remainder, and hence, "No object is wholly known."[66] Piaget would agree with this assumption (which is actually Kantian),[67] but he would lament the situation. Biological systems, he notes, which fulfill primary needs such as food and protection, must remain "open" because "the organism only succeeds in preserving its form through a continuous flow of exchanges with the environment."[68] But "an open system is a system that is perpetually threatened."[69] In contrast, cognitive systems tend toward "closure": by registering environmental feedback, they form a circular structure which gives the organism power to regulate and control exchanges with the environment.[70]

Yet insofar as cognitive structures cannot be divorced from their content — and any language act that intends meaning is an example of this — such closure must remain incomplete. Piaget finds only one exception among cognitive structures, the closed system of mathematical logic, that "structure of structures" for which he has such a strong predilection:

> Logico-mathematical structures do, in fact, present us with an example, to be found nowhere else in creation, of a development which evolves without a break . . . . [71]

Adorno considered this predilection for closed systems (the mark of idealist philosophy) in fact not so very far from the animalism which it strove to overcome. Abstract reason, he claimed, tends literally to gobble everything up, so that nothing is left outside. Ultimately, all of material nature is consumed without a trace — as is in fact the case with mathematics. Adorno wrote, using his own biological metaphors:

> The system in which the sovereign mind imagined itself transfigured, has its primal history in the pre-mental, the animal life of the species.

> Predators get hungry, but pouncing on their prey is difficult and often
> dangerous; additional impulses may be needed for the beast to dare it.
> These impulses and the unpleasantness of hunger fuse into rage at the vic-
> tim . . . .
>
> The animal to be devoured must be evil . . . and finally all that
> reminds us of nature is inferior, so the unity of the self-preserving thought
> may devour it without misgivings. This justifies the principle of the
> thought as much as it increases the appetite. The system is the belly turn-
> ed mind, and rage is the mark of each and every idealism.[72]

In this sophisticated version of Topsy-Turvies, Adorno then points out
that, just as the logic of mathematics reflects the structure of abstract exchange and mathematics becomes a metaphor for commercial society, so
thought as a "closed system," far from independent or uncontaminated by
matter, "really approximated" the system of the social world to which the
individual is forced to conform, where "less and less was left outside."[73]

Children use language to construct nonsense worlds that protest against
the limits of reality by transgressing them. But they also protect reality
against the tyranny of language. In the form of riddles, language jokes and
puns, a persistent and apparently spontaneous form of children's play,[74]
children are in complicity with objects, rescuing them from being consumed by the concept. These language games function because of the ambivalence of referents, the fact that the word doesn't identify the object
totally.

What's black and white and red all over?
A newspaper.

What goes up the chimney down, but not down the chimney up?
An umbrella.

In riddles, only when the object slips out of the meaning first anticipated
by the question is sense restored. Puns, double entendres, and all am-
bivalences which emerge in the gap between signifier and signified are thus
an occasion for the practice of dialectical operations.

Adorno referred to his own method as "riddle-solving,"[75] and the name
was apt. He analyzed spoken or written words as if they were puzzles or
hieroglyphs. Their meanings were ambivalent, not identical to the
speaker's own conscious intent. They were thus in need of a dialectical interpretation which could compensate for the limits of the concept by
grasping truth at contradictory levels.[76]

If we apply this kind of hermeneutical method to the statements of

children, they take on significance as critical insights into reality. This text
is given to us by Piaget's daughter:

> At 3; 11 (12): *"that little baby was bought. They found her in a shop
> and bought her."* . . . At 5; 3 (23), referring to the guinea-pigs she had
> just been given to help her to discover the true solution: *"Where do little
> guinea-pigs come from? —* What do you think? *— From a factory."* . . . At
> 5; 5 (8): *"Were the little guinea-pigs inside their mother? I think they
> were."* But two days later: "They come from the factory."[77]

For Piaget, this text exemplifies a "mythic" stage of "artificialism,"[78] a
set of wrong answers on the path toward scientific understanding. Yet what
the child is quite accurately reflecting is the ambivalence between natural
and social sources of the materially-given objects of experience. The persistence of the child in connecting creation to the social process, first in
terms of store-bought commodities and then in terms of factory production, may be more on the right track than off.

The question of origins is a question of creation as well as causality, and
here the contradiction is between the concept of creation as a conscious
product of human activity, to quote Marx, an "act of self-creation,"[79] and
the reality of alienated labor, characterized by dependency on another to
whom (again from Marx) "I owe . . . not only the maintenance of my life
but also its *creation,* its *source.* My life necessarily has such an external
ground if it is not my own creation."[80] To make is to be a subject; to be
made is to be an object. This much Piaget's daughter knew:

> At 5; 5 (22): ". . . What things make themselves? — *Pipes, trees, egg-
> shells, clouds, the door. They don't make themselves, they have to be
> made. I think trees make themselves, and suns too. In the sky they can
> easily make themselves."* At 5; 7 (11): *"How is the sky made? I think they
> cut it out. It's been painted."* At 5; 7 (12): *"How do they make stones?
> How do they hold together? How are they made? . . . —I think it's with
> cement."* At 5; 7 (22), on seeing the sun set behind a mountain ridge: *"So
> the sun moves too, does it? Like the moon? Somebody makes it moves
> (sic), somebody behind the mountain, a giant, I think."*[81]

The confusion in the child's mind between making and being made
reflects a real condition. It is not just the figment of a 5 year old imagination. The child's "artificialism," the transformation of objects into subjects, is a human inversion of the original distortion, the social transformation of subjects into objects. Such "wrong" answers are reflections of
utopia, that form of Topsy Turvies which would set the world aright. An

interpretation which recognizes that this not only describes the child's learning, but learns from it.

Language and Society: The Image of the Trickster

Advanced levels of negative, dialectical operations can be distinguished from the more elementary puns and language jokes in that they involve whole texts, whole structures of meanings rather than individual words, as they relate to the social structure rather than individual objects. It is with some misgivings that at this point I bring Jürgen Habermas into the discussion. For unlike Adorno, his colleague in the 1960s at the Frankfurt *Institut für Sozialforschung,* Habermas, a powerful and complex theorist in his own right, has expressly addressed himself to the work of Piaget and Kohlberg, incorporating elements of both in his work with rather less criticism than I am voicing here.[82] Moreover, Habermas has rejected Adorno's relentless negativity and worked out a positive dialectical theory of ego development in which "identity" is not a pejorative term and in which ontogenetic and phylogenetic parallels produce strong Hegelian reverberations.[83] But if I may borrow eclectically from Habermas (given his own extraordinary eclecticism, this seems only fair play), when applied to the relation between structures of meanings and social structures, his theory of communicative action can be illuminating.

That theory focuses on a central contradiction in the speech situation. Implied in speaking is a reciprocity of understanding between speaker and listener, the pre-requisite for a possible consensus of meaing. This mutuality has the structure of democratic equality, yet within present society it remains a utopian hope.[84] For if the structure of the social relationship between speaker and listener is one of domination, true reciprocity is impossible, and the act of communication itself will be distorted.

There is a Finnish *schwank* which expresses this contradiction clearly. To understand its humor is to grasp Habermas' problematic:

> Well, once a farmer and his servant were starting their meal, as the neighbors were eating too. So the farmer said "Let's pretend eating, but not eat." The servant contented himself with it, and then when they went to the field to mow, the servant took the blade off the scythe and said "Now let's pretend mowing, but not mow."[85]

The democratic structure of the language exchange, emphasized metaphorically by the parallel sentence structure, suggests an equality that doesn't exist. It is out of phase with the structure of domination between master and servant, and this non-identity provides the occasion for the humor of the servant's trick. This trickster who tears the veil from the apparent reciprocity of the speech exchange is the prototype of the social critic.

The trickster is a seminal figure in folk literature, from the Homeric Hymn to the tales of Uncle Remus. Tricks differ from crimes because they do not betray the shared bond of human communication and hence its utopian promise, but instead play on the ambivalence of meanings,[86] acknowledging the rules of the game but turning the tables, using those rules against the game itself. The trickster lives above and beneath social constraints as well as within them. He demonstrates that the question of who controls the relations between signifier and signified in the production of meanings is a political question; and, although he acts to save his own skin, in using language to outwit the powerful, he is clearly the ally of the powerless. As is true of Uncle Remus's Brer Rabbit stories, "it is not virtue that triumphs, but helplessness."[87] As the inventor of meanings, the trickster is the prototype not only of the social critic, but of the artist or paradigm-breaking scientist as well. Uncle Remus comments:

> One of the reasons that made old Brer Rabbit get along so well was that he never copies any of the other creatures. When he made his disappearance before them it was always in some brand new place.[88]

Yet despite the revolutionary potential of the trickster, he is tolerated by the powerful so long as he remains at the peripheries of society where he can in fact function as an aid to social stability. Kerényi writes:

> Disorder belongs to the totality of life, and the spirit of this disorder is the trickster. His function . . . is to add disorder to order and so make a whole, to render possible, within the fixed bounds of what is permitted, an experience of what is not permitted.[89]

In the Roman Saturnalia, masters served slaves, but the topsy-turvy world of the Carnival owed its very meaning to the fact that it was an extraordinary event; hence it served to define the boundaries of the real social world all the more precisely. The trickster is one of many cases of fringe figures—witches, magicians, fools, prophets—whose potentially revolutionary behavior is socialized within abnormal occasions of festival and ritual.[90] Their powers limited to a peripheral realm, they act as buffers or mediators against the natural and supernatural worlds. Hence prophets inhabit the wilderness;[91] and to accuse someone of withcraft is "the political idiom of out-casting and re-definition of social boundaries."[92]

The crucial question is one of legitimacy: these figures and the classes of social "underdogs" they represent must themselves acquiesce to the peripheral position which established authority allots to them. When medieval ideology condemned usury as a sin, so long as medieval capitalists accepted the Church's meaning of their activity, they could not challenge the nobles' political power:

> The medieval merchant accepted his own equation with the thief: he carried a thief's thumb as a talisman to help him in his business, shared his patron Saint Nicholas with the thief, and made Reynard the Fox [a famous trickster] his hero and ideal.[93]

But in periods of social disequilibrium, when the "normal" world has itself gone topsy-turvy, fringe figures may suddenly become central. Then witches call themselves visionaries, prophets turn into messiahs, and tricksters shed their masks of humor and are revealed as heroes.[94] When the legitimacy of the powerful is undermined (a threat endemic to late capitalist societies, if we are to believe Habermas),[95] then objects escape the domination of old concepts and the world can be renamed. The cognitive method of Adorno (himself very like a trickster) is relevant in this context because it entails a shift in vision so that "apocryphal realms on the edges of civilization move suddenly into the center."[96] The dialectical reversal of meanings inherent in his method, what Nietzsche called a transvaluation of values, is no new invention. The seventeenth-century Jewish mystic Sabbatai Zevi claimed himself to be the Messiah by converting to Islam, and averred that in the Messianic age, "everyone who wants to serve God as he does now . . . [will] be called a desecrator . . . " and what is now considered sinful will become a holy act.[97] The revolutionary message of Marxism is not different:

> Under the dictatorship of the proletariat the relationship between legality and illegality undergoes a change in function, for now what was formerly legal becomes illegal and vice versa.[98]

The dialectics of critical humor, expressed in the *schwank* by the servant's trick against the master, keeps the utopian moment alive within speech even when within reality it may appear to have vanished. But Hegel's story of the dialectic between master and slave,[99] which begins humorlessly with a fight unto death (a struggle, it should be noted, for the same mutual recognition which underlies Habermas' notion of communicative action), goes further than illuminating the gap between language and reality: it renames reality by reversing the relation between signifiers and signified, and in so doing illuminates the logic of social transformation: the slave realizes that as the active producer, he is in fact the master, while the master, totally dependent on another's labor, is the slave; the only way out of the vicious circle whereby masters end up slaves is to eradicate the hierarchical structure altogether, so that social relations really become a reciprocity between equals, and reality thus lives up to the utopian promise of language.

Dialectics and the Child's World

The argument that a genetic epistemology should focus its attention on dialectical, cognitive operations rather than abstract, formal ones is based, not on grounds of political expediency, but on the premise that it comes closer to truth. (In this case the right theoretical tendency and the right political tendency converge.)[100] In order to comprehend reality, children need to be able to think dialectically, because the world of their experience is in fact dialectically structured. Moreover, the child's development is composed of precisely that tension between domination and submission, power and helplessness, independence and dependence which forms the central contradiction of the larger social structure.

The fundamental paradox of children's existence is that they desire autonomy yet are dependent on adults. In order to gain power over their own environment, children give up a false sense of omnipotence and submit to the authority of the powerful—first their parents, then their teachers. By submitting to adults' tutelage, children acquire the knowledge and power to rebel against them. Piaget recognizes that learning is motivated by the child's respect for "an adult who has personal authority," and gives rise to "imitation of the superior by the subordinate."[101] Hegel clearly implies a parallel between the dialectic of master and slave and the relation between teacher and student: submitting to authority is necessary in the process of developing intellectual independence.[102] And the correlation between childhood and social powerlessness has long been recognized by myths in which the socially impotent are represented in the image of the child. Just as the Messiah comes with the birth of a baby, so when Hermes becomes identified with the lower class struggle against the aristocracy, he first appears in myth as a new-born child.[103]

Children themselves, of course, are at first unaware of the connection. Their struggle against authority, which begins in the second year against the mother and continues, involving the father in the 4 year old Oedipal phase, is a private one, and is not correlated with any objective comprehension of the class structure of society.[104] The association between their own helplessness and that of the poor or socially outcast is instead made for them by adults. It is conveyed to them through fairy tales.

If myths project social inequalities onto the image of the child, then fairy tales do just the opposite: they project the child's experience of inferiority onto a social image.[105] Children are encouraged to identify in fairy tales with paupers who become princes, youths who slay ogres, poor men who become rich, and to see in these allegories the possibility for their own transformation.[106]

Fairy tales are complex phenomena. To unravel their enigma, to separate their several layers of meaning as a dialogue between generations, would indeed provide a model for a dialectical developmental psychology. Fairy tales are for children but not *of* children: "the child knows about fairyland only what the adult tells him."[107] Told within a context of "vertical inequality between parents and children,"[108] they require a categorical distinction between generations which in Western civilization, as Ariès tells us, was a relatively late invention, a discovery of the seventeenth-century bourgeoisie.[109] The fairy tale brings pleasure to adult and child alike, but surely not for the same reasons. (The child's own narrative constructions have a different logic.) The adult, with first-hand knowledge of the inequities and inadequacies of the social order, has the chance in telling the tale to make that order different, reconstructing the world in a more utopian form.[110] The child who hears the story discovers in terms of a social allegory the logical possibility of resolving his own existential paradox — indeed, with the aid and abetting of those very authorities whose domination he desires to overcome. Thus the fairy tale is a constellation in which, for the moment, the utopian reconciliation of generational conflict and social conflict converge in one image.

Yet the image is an illusion, the projections a distortion. Were it otherwise, then every adult who told a fairy tale and every child who listened would support the socially oppressed. Despite parallels, the fusion of the dialectics of child and pauper entails a confusion of nature and history which camouflages their real difference. Specifically: (1) Childhood is a state which is outgrown naturally, as are those forms of helplessness, dependency and inferiority peculiar to that state: "vertical inequality is always surmounted in reality. Life will transform all children into adults."[111] This inevitably happy ending is not guaranteed in the social history of oppression; and (2) When children become adults, they invariably reproduce the structure of inequality with respect to the next generation. This need not be true of relations between people in social reality.

In the dialectics of domination, the structures of class struggle and the Oedipal situation have formal parallels, but they are out of phase with each other. They exist on different axes, class and generation, which intersect in a variety of specific constellations,[112] but do not lose their particularity by merging into one: Marrying happily ever after will get you out of the Oedipal bind but not the social one; waging proletarian revolution will get you out of the class bind but not the generational one. Because the individual's struggle does not translate into the social struggle without leaving a remainder, it follows that: (1) It will not do to interpret domination only as a problem of natural history, to dismiss the political act of regicide as an Oedipal projection, or to reduce social revolution to a struggle against paternal authority. Political and social oppression have an independent and objective reality. Not only guilt motivates the pact of fraternity or comradeship (as Freud argued in *Moses and Monotheism*), but rational awareness of the dialectical contradiction within the master-slave relationship which afflicts master as well as slave and is not resolved by a reversal of terms, but only if the hierarchical structure itself is overcome; and (2) It will not do to see class struggle simply as a problem of social history. The "worker" in Marxist theory is a remarkably static, reified concept, one that forgets origins, the natural history of the child who becomes a worker. Here Piaget's developmental perspective on consciousness (as well as Freud's on the unconscious) provides a necessary correction of Marx.

Lévi-Strauss argues that both the tale of Oedipus and the theory of class struggle can be merged within the metamyth of a mathematical formula.[113] Our approach would be the reverse: rather than merging them into one, they should be kept at a distance, so that each can be used to demythify the other. Not to do so can result in intellectual error, a case of mixed metaphors where the trick is on us, and rather than controlling the production of meanings, we end up controlled by them. A text from Piaget illustrates this:

> The conflict between obedience and individual liberty is, for example, the affliction of childhood, and in real life the only solutions to this conflict are submission, revolt, or cooperation which involves some measure of compromise.[114]

Piaget's description of the child's conflict as one between "obedience and individual liberty" is really the description of the conflict between individual and state in bourgeois society: the dialectical paradox is that in order to be free, one has to obey certain laws. This indeed parallels the child's dilemma: in order to become autonomous, he or she needs to submit to parental authority. But to talk about "compromise" and "cooperation" in the child's case is really a euphemism, because of children's natural inferiority, while citizens of a democracy, in theory at least, are themselves the origin of the laws which constrain them. On the other hand, insofar as bourgeois democracies do not live up to their concept because of the persistence of structural inequalities on the social level, the condition of oppressed social groups really does resemble that of childhood. By ignoring those unequal power relations which are one of the "afflictions of childhood," Piaget speaks the ideology of his own political system, in which "compromise," as mutually reciprocal agreement, implies a relation between equals that does not exist: "Compromise" has the same distorted meaning when applied to a labor arbitration where workers call for $3.00 an hour, management $2.50, and settlement is made at $2.75 (or when the electorate concedes to the victory of candidate A over candidate B, neither of whom represents its interest) as it does when applied to the case of parents offering their child the choice: "All right, do you want to wash your ears and then brush your teeth, or brush your teeth and then wash your ears?"

But to claim that the structure of society prevents democracy from "living up to its concept" is really too weak to describe the seriousness — and the absurdity — of the child's world in the present historical era. Over the fundamental contradiction of class there hangs the shadow of another paradox, that the industrialized, militarized reality to which children must adapt in order to survive increasingly threatens survival. Moreover, those with power are as helpless as those without to escape the life-endangering consequences of that reality.

In Vonnegut's novel, *Cat's Cradle*, Philip Castle tells the story of the time the bubonic plague hit the tropical town of San Lorenzo where his father had founded a hospital. If the plague can be seen as a symbol of the destructive potential of the present world order, then the story can be read as a modern *schwank*, expressing the paradox of today's master class:

> "When the plague was having everything its own way, the House of Hope and Mercy in the Jungle looked like Auschwitz or Buchenwald. We had stacks of dead so deep and wide that a bulldozer actually stalled try-

ing to shove them toward a common grave. Father worked without sleep
for days, worked not only without sleep but without saving many lives
either."

* * * * *

". . . one sleepless night I stayed up with Father while he worked. It
was all we could do to find a live patient to treat. In bed after bed after
bed we found dead people.

"And Father started giggling," Castle continued.

"He couldn't stop. He walked out into the night with his flashlight. He
was still giggling. He was making the flashlight beam dance over all the
dead people stacked outside. He put his hand on my head, and do you
know what that marvelous man said to me?" asked Castle.

"Nope."

" 'Son,' my father said to me, 'someday this will all be yours.' "[115]

Conclusion

. . . the object of a mental experience is an antagonistic system in
itself—antagonistic in reality, not just in its conveyance to the knowing
subject that rediscovers itself therein. . . . Regarding the concrete
possibility of utopia, dialectics is the ontology of the wrong state of things.
The right state of things would be free of it: neither a system nor a contradiction.[116]

Fairy tales provide an image in which non-identicals are fused, and in this
imag-ining which reconstructs reality there exists a utopian promise. But
the other pole of that promise is critical thinking that demythifies reality:
here non-identicals converge only when, as concepts (children and oppressed, tricksters and heroes, masters and slaves), they are held apart.
Fundamental to both fantasy and critical negation (as well as to humor) is
the linguistic representation of the non-identity between thought and reality. The abstract formalism of Piaget's cognitive structures reflects the
abstract formalism of the social structure, and this is the source of their
truth. But it is less adequate than dialectical thinking, because it cannot
reflect critically upon itself, and because it cannot capture the ambivalence between the egalitarianism implied by abstract exchange and
the social structures of domination in which that exchange takes place.

If there were a shift in focus from formal to dialectical operations, the
new generation might indeed be encouraged to develop dialectical skills,
for the hierarchical relation between adults and children tends to evoke in
the latter what is looked for by the former. No one need fear, however,

that this would mean raising a generation of revolutionaries. It is not social criticism which causes social disequilibrium, and the source of society's disorders lies elsewhere than in cognitive structures. But what might be hoped for is a new generation with the intellectual tools for comprehending change and the shifting of meanings which it entails, and with the cognitive independence, now reserved for a few, to be themselves producers of meaning. In the face of social disequilibrium, such a generation would not need to escape from the freedom that would be released. Rather than clutching at crusts of an old order, or being led blindly by demagogues into a new one, they could cultivate the creative potential of change, and the utopian possibilities of renaming the world.

References
*For Klaus Riegel, 1925-1977.

1 Walter Benjamin, "Über den Begriff der Geschichte," in *Gesammelte Schriften,* 6 vols., eds. Rolf Tiedemann and Hermann Schweppenhäser, vol. 1:2, *Abhandlungen* (Frankfurt am Main: Suhrkamp Verlag, 1974), pp. 693-694.

2 Theodor W. Adorno, *Negative Dialectics,* trans. E. B. Ashton (New York: The Seabury Press, 1973), p. 15.

3 Susan Buck-Morss, "Socio-economic Bias in Piaget's Theory and its Implications for Cross-Culture Studies," *Human Development* 18 (1975): 35-49. Republished in Klaus F. Riegel, ed., *The Development of Dialectical Operations* (Basil, Switzerland: Karger, 1975).

4 For an overview of the cross-cultural controversy and research, see P. R. Dasen, "Cross-cultural Piagetian Research: A Summary," *Journal of Cross-Cultural Psychology 3,* 1 (1972): 23-39.

5 Georg Lukács, *History and Class Consciousness,* first published in German, 1923, trans. Rodney Livingstone (Cambridge, Mass.: The MIT Press, 1971).

6 In considering cognitive development as an analogy to biological evolution Piaget acknowledges that objects might themselves influence the development of mathematical cognitive structures, and recognizes that if objects really influenced subjective structures, "my interpretation would need some rather basic revision. It would just be one of those unfortunate things that happen . . . . " Cf. Jean Piaget, *Biology and Knowledge: An Essay on the Relations between Organic Regulations and Cognitive Processes* (Chicago: The University of Chicago Press, 1971), p. 342.

7 For a more detailed analysis of that method, see Susan Buck-Morss, *The Origin*

of Negative Dialectics: Theodor W. Adorno, Walter Benjamin, and the Frankfurt Institute (New York: Macmillan Free Press, 1977).

8 Lawrence Kohlberg, "Stage and Sequence: The Cognitive-Developmental Approach to Socialization," in Goslin, ed., *Handbook of Socialization Theory and Research* (Chicago: Rand McNally, 1969), p. 452.

9 In mental development "successive constructions always involve a decentering of the initial egocentric point of view in order to place it in an ever-broader coordination of relations and concepts, so that each new terminal grouping further integrates the subject's activity by adapting it to an ever-widening reality." Ultimately this entails submission to social constraints. Piaget continues: "Parallel to this intellectual elaboration, we have seen affectivity gradually disengaging itself from the self in order to submit, thanks to the reciprocity and coordination of values, to the laws of cooperation." Cf. Jean Piaget, "The Mental Development of the Child," *Six Psychological Studies,* introd. David Elkind, trans. Anita Tenzer (New York: Random House, 1967), p. 69.

10 Piaget's affinity to Kant is also clear in his "constructivism," that is, his stress on the moment of the subject's spontaneous activity in cognition which is the hallmark of Kantian philosophy. For a discussion of the connection between Kantian thinking and socio-political reality after 1848, see Buck-Morss, *The Origin of Negative Dialectics,* pp. 70-71.

11 Adorno, *Negative Dialectics,* p. xx.

12 Kant said reality is what it is because of man's perception of it; Adorno said man's perception is what it is because of reality's structure: "The fetish character of commodities is no fact of consciousness, but dialectic in the emanating sense that it produces consciousness." Cf. Adorno's letter to Walter Benjamin, August 2, 1935, in Theodor W. Adorno, *Über Walter Benjamin* (Frankfurt am Main: Suhrkamp Verlag, 1970), p. 112.

13 Piaget, "Genesis and Structure in the Psychology of Intelligence," *Six Psychological Studies,* p. 151.

14 James Youniss, "Operations and Everyday Thinking: A commentary on 'Dialectical Operations.' " *Human Development* 17 (1974): 388-389.

15 Cf. Georg Lukács, "What is Orthodox Marxism?" *History and Class Consciousness,* pp. 1-26.

16 Cf. Max Horkheimer, "Hegel und das Problem der Metaphysik," *Festschrift für Carl Grünberg: Zum 70. Geburtstag* (Leipzig: Verlag von C. L. Hirschfeld, 1932).

17 Cf. Susan Buck-Morss, *The Origin of Negativae Dialectics,* p. 48.

18 For a discussion of Adorno's criticism of reality not living up to its concept, see *Ibid.,* pp. 43-62.

19 *Ibid.,* pp. 185-186.

20 Adorno admitted that his theory was a kind of mental acrobatics, an intellectual free-fall, not without occasional sensations of vertigo due to the lack of firm ground under one's mental toes. (Adorno, *Negative Dialectics,* pp. 31-34).

21 When Adorno illuminates the historical "source" of a phenomenon it is by reconstructing the past as it makes a constellation with the present, so that the historical prototype of a persent phenomenon becomes visible. Riegel (citing Meacham and Kvale) makes a similar point in his paper on biographies: the individual constantly reinterprets his past life in light of the present, so that "any new experience alters the structure of memory . . . . " Cf. Klaus F. Riegel, "The Dialectics of Time," in *Life-span Developmental Psychology,* eds. H. Datan and H. W. Reese (New York: Academic Press, 1977).

22 Bloom has suggested that every act of writing (creation) and reading (interpretation) is a metaphorical substitution or "misreading" of a preceding text: each is a re-presentation or re-seeing of tradition whereby the present generation frees itself from the domination of ancestors by joining them. Here the point of "origin" is the past source of present creativity, not a prior cause to which the present can be mechanistically reduced. Cf. Harold Bloom, *A Map of Misreading* (New York: Oxford University Press, 1975).

23 Susan Buck-Morss, The Origin of Negative Dialectics, pp. 49-50.

24 "Perhaps from early on in the bourgeois era the experiment became a surrogate for authentic experience." From Theodor W. Adorno, *Notizen zur neuen Anthropologie* (Frankfurt am Main: Adorno Estate, 1942).

25 Paul Collaer, *A History of Modern Music,* trans. Sally Abeles (New York: The World Publishing Company, 1961), p. 68.

26 Cited in Germaine Brée, *Marcel Proust and Deliverance from Time,* trans. C. J. Richards and A. D. Truitt (New Brunswick, N. J.: Rutgers University Press, 1969), p. 55.

27 Theodor W. Adorno, "Charakteristik Walter Benjamins," *Über Walter Benjamin,* p. 14.

28 In fairness to Piaget, his theoretical discoveries were based on an open, decidedly creative method of research which made use of a small sample with whom he was
very much involved (his own children) and which thus violated some fundamental
ground rules of "scientific" methodology. But in the standardized application of
Piagetian tests, consistency rather than discovery has become the criterion for
truth. For a revealing criticism of this testing by a psychologist who experimented
with 1,400 children in three countries, see J. Smedslund, "Piaget's Psychology in
Practice," *British Journal of Educational Psychology* 47 (1977): 1-6.

29 Cf. Jean Piaget, *Biology and Knowledge.*

30 Cf. Colin Murray Turbayne, *The Myth of Metaphor,* revised edition (Colum-
bia, South Carolina: University of South Carolina Press, 1970).

31 Emile Durkheim and Marcel Mauss, *Primitive Classification,* trans. Rodney
Livingstone (Chicago: University of Chicago Press, 1963), p. 71.

32 Michael Polanyi, *Personal Knowledge* (Chicago: University of Chicago Press,
1958), p. 291.

33 Cited in E. Duckworth, "Piaget Rediscovered," *Journal of Research in the
Science of Teaching* 2 (1964): 175.

34 Cf. Gouldner's distinction (building on T. S. Kuhn's theory of paradigms)
between intellectuals and conventional scholars: "Intellectuals, then, are scholars
who reject, make problematic, or critically focalize the boundaries hitherto implicit
in normal scholarship and the scholarly paradigms on which the scholarly community had, till then, centered, and their elaborated speech variants. Searching
out and transcending the conventional boundaries of 'normal scholarship,' they are
an irritant to conventional scholars, who condemn them as deviants. Rather than
operating safely within the familiar boundaries of an established paradigm, intellectuals violate boundaries. They mingle once separate disciplines; they pass
back and forth between ordinary and artificial languages; between the 'common
sense' and technical tradition. Such boundary transgressions sometimes generate
scandalous intellectual *incunabala;* but, sometimes, they are the basis of powerful
intellectual breakthroughs and of rich innovations." Cf. Alvin W. Gouldner, "Pro-
logue to a Theory of Revolutionary Intellectuals," *Telos* 26, Winter 1975-76: 23.

35 Cf. Jean Piaget, *To Understand is to Invent: The Future of Education* (New
York: Grossman Publishers, 1973). Although Piaget stresses the active role of the
subject in cognition (p. 18), here as elsewhere, invention is in fact no more than the
"rediscovery of truth" (p. 34).

36 Piaget rejects Freud's definition of play as the domination of the pleasure principle over the reality principle, noting that the repetition of even painful experiences is a "primary factor in play and more widespread than the pursuit of
pleasure for its own sake." Cf. Jean Piaget, *Play, Dreams and Imitation in
Childhood,* trans. C. Gattegno and F. M. Hodgson (New York: W. W. Norton and
Company, 1962), p. 149. Note also that Adorno, while arguing that fantasy as an
aesthetic experience is never an escape from reality, affirms Freud's radical
dichotomy between the physical desire for gratification and its forced repression by
the overly constraining structure of present reality. Adorno claimed that art expresses the individual's fantasy of omnipotence, not as controller of existing reality,
but as creator of utopian possibility, "the wish within the artwork for constructing a
better world." Cf. Theodor W. Adorno, *Gesammelte Schriften,* 23 vols., eds. Rolf
Tiedemann and Gretel Adorno, vol. 7: *Aesthetische Theorie* (Frankfurt am Main:
Suhrkamp Verlag, 1970), p. 22; also pp. 19-31.

37 Jean Piaget, *Play, Dreams and Imitation in Childhood,* p. 150.

38 *Ibid.,* p. 149.

39 *Ibid.,* p. 89.

40 *Ibid.,* p. 90.

41 *Ibid.,* p. 149.

42 ". . . play is distinguishable by a modification, varying in degree, of the conditions of equilibrium between reality and the ego. We can therefore say that if
adapted activity and thought constitute an equilibrium between assimilation and
accommodation, play begins as soon as there is predominance of assimilation."
(*Ibid.,* p. 150).

43 The distinction between negative dialectics and the positive dialectics which the
system of Hegelian idealism has in common with the "vulgar" Marxism of, for example, Engels' *Dialectics of Nature* (which has become the basis for official Soviet
Marxism) is that in both the latter the stress is on the reconciliation of contradictions by an automatic process in which the cognitive efforts of the subject become
predictable. In negative, or critical dialectics, the aim is not to resolve contradictions, but to contradict resolutions. Note Riegel's definition: "rather than searching
for final answers, dialectical logic is concerned with the origin of the endless sequence of raising questions." Cf. Klaus F. Riegel, "From Traits and Equilibrium
Toward Developmental Dialectics," *1975 Nebraska Symposium on Motivation,* ed.
W. J. Arnold (Lincoln: University of Nebraska Press, 1976), p. 372.

44 Riegel argues that tolerance of ambiguity represents a more developed cognitive stage. Cf. Klaus F. Riegel, "Dialectical Operations: The Final Period of Cognitive Development," *Human Development* 16 (1973): 356. Although in that article Riegel was considering dialectical operations only as a late stage of development, I am quite sure he would have agreed with the spirit of the project outlined here.

45 Piaget describes fully-developed spatial comprehension thus: "the construction results in a universe of permanent objects constituting a single practical space that is relatively decentered (in that it includes the child's own body as one element among many) . . . . " Cf. Jean Piaget, *Play, Dreams and Imitation in Childhood,* p. 262.

46 A Necker cube (see Fig. 1) is transparent with one shaded side that can be read alternately as the foremost and hindmost plane of the cube: It may be noted that spatial ambivalence in designs existed in very early cultures. Lévi-Strauss comments that the art of several Indian cultures in North and South America is "marked by an intellectual delight in double-meanings (in Hopewell [Eastern USA], as in Chavin [north of Peru], certain motifs bear one meaning when read normally, and quite another when read upside-down)." Cf. Claude Lévi-Strauss, *Tristes Tropiques* (New York: Atheneum, 1964), p. 246.

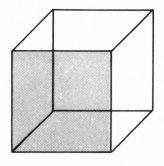

Fig. 1

47 See Jean Piaget and Bärbel Inhelder, *The Child's Conception of Space* (London: Routledge & Kegan Paul, 1955).

48 This might in fact be a continued development of skills in "intellectual realism" (described in *ibid.*) which Piaget considers Stage 2 (ages 4-7 years), and claims is superceded by "visual realism," i.e., the capacity to draw with perspective.

49 Jean Piaget, *The Child's Concept of Time*, trans. A. J. Pomerans (London: Routledge & Kegan Paul, 1969), p. 2.

50 Adorno considered the stereotyped syncopation employed in popular jazz no real negation of standard rhythms because it was "purposeless; it leads nowhere, and is arbitrarily revoked through a dialectical, mathematical conversion of time-counts which leaves no remainder." Cf. Theodor W. Adorno, "Über Jazz" (1936) *Moments Musicaux: Neugedruckte Aufsätze, 1928 bis 1962* (Frankfurt am Main: Suhrkamp Verlag, 1964), p. 112.

51 *Ibid.*

52 In testing the child's concept of time, for example, Piaget investigates rhythmic perception. But true to his bias, he utilizes a metronome, which provides an abstract measurement of rhythms (motions relative to an absolute, formal time) rather than rhythms as they appear within a musical content which gives them meaning. Or, testing comprehension of two simultaneous motions of varying velocities (in our example, left-hand triplets counterposed to right-hand couplets), Piaget searches for the child's comprehension of identity, rather than non-identity, i.e., the fact that "total durations are equal" despite varying velocities. Cf. Jean Piaget, *The Child's Concept of Time*, p. 170.

53 For Piaget's discussion of the "fundamental problem" concerning the nature and origin of Chomsky's "fixed innate schema," and his proposed way out of this theoretical difficulty (that language structures are derived from concrete operations, and these produce structures which are neither wholly innate nor wholly acquired, but discovered through experience), cf. Jean Piaget, *Structuralism*, trans. and ed., Chaninah Maschler (New York: Harper Torchbooks, 1970), pp. 81-96.

54 Jean Piaget, "Language and Thought from the Genetic Point of View," in *Six Psychological Studies*, p. 98.

55 Piaget, *Structuralism*, p. 74.

56 Piaget, "Language and Thought from the Genetic Point of View," in *Six Psychological Studies*, pp. 92-93.

57 "The fact is that adults think in terms of allegories and metaphors, whereas children think in terms of objects perceived in their world of objects. Their thinking is limited during the first years to images of things . . . . I know of a 4 year old child who gets furious whenever she hears an adult speak about ladyfinger biscuits." Cf. Kornei Chukovsky, *From Two to Five*, trans. and ed. Miriam Morton (Berkeley: University of California Press, 1974), pp. 12-13.

58 Cf. Susan Buck-Morss, *The Origin of Negative Dialectics*, pp. 88-89.

59 *Ibid.*, pp. 89-90.

60 Cited in Chukovsky, *From Two to Five*, p. 96.

61 *Ibid.*, p. 110. Like Adorno, Chukovsky considered creativity a common component of art and science.

62 *Ibid.*, p. 61.

63 *Ibid.*, p. 95.

64 Cited in *ibid.*, p. 99.

65 *Ibid.*, p. 98.

66 Adorno, *Negative Dialectics*, p. 14.

67 It is Kant's distinction between reality (noumena) and appearance (phenomena). The noumenal realm of "things-in-themselves" forever escapes us, for we can only know objects as phenomena, as they appear to us in cognitive experience, through the grid of subjectivity.

68 Piaget, *Biology and Knowledge*, p. 350.

69 *Ibid.*

70 *Ibid.*, p. 354.

71 *Ibid.*, p. 355.

72 Theodor W. Adorno, *Negative Dialectics*, p. 22-23.

73 *Ibid.*, p. 23. "If society could be seen through as a closed system, a system accordingly unreconciled to the subjects, it would become too embarrassing for the subjects as long as they remain subjects in any sense." (*Ibid.*, p. 24).

74 Cf. Iona and Peter Opie, *The Lore and Language of Schoolchildren* (Oxford: The Clarendon Press, 1959).

75 Theodor W. Adorno, "Die Aktualität der Philosophie," *Gesammelte Schriften*, vol. 1: *Philosophische Frühschriften*, ed. Rolf Tiedemann (Frankfurt am Main: Suhrkamp Verlag, 1973), pp. 334-335.

76 "The determinable flaw in every concept makes it necessary to cite others; this is the font of the only constellations which inherited some of the hope of the name." Cf. Theodor W. Adorno, *Negative Dialectics*, p. 53.

77 Cited in Jean Piaget, *Play, Dreams and Imitation in Childhood*, pp. 246-247.

78 *Ibid.*, p. 250.

79 Karl Marx, "Economic and Philosophic Manuscripts," in *Writings of the Young Marx on Philosophy and Society*, trans. and ed. Loyd D. Easton and Kurt H. Guddat (Garden City, N. Y.: Doubleday/Anchor Books, 1967), p. 332.

80 *Ibid.*, pp. 312-313.

81 Jean Piaget, *Play, Dreams and Imitation in Childhood*, p. 248.

82 Cf., for example, Jürgen Habermas, "Das Rollenkonzept des Sozialisationsvorganges," *Kultur und Kritik: Verstreute Aufsätze* (Frankfurt am Main: Suhrkamp Verlag, 1973), pp. 118-194.

83 Jürgen Habermas, "Moral Development and Ego Identity," trans. George Ellard, *Telos* 24 (Summer 1975): 41-55.

84 Adorno, who had an overriding concern for the individual, never directly addressed the question of intersubjective communication. It could be said that for him the work of art was the expression of utopian hope, indeed, on the same grounds of "domination-free communication" which Habermas posited for communicative action. As Adorno wrote: "Artworks say we." (Theodor W. Adorno, *Gesammelte Schriften*, vol. 7: *Aesthetische Theorie*, p. 250).

85 Discussed in Elli-Kaija Köngas, "A Finnish Schwank Pattern: The Farmer-Servant Cycle of the Kuusisto Family," *Midwest Folklore* 11 (1962): 210.

86 A favorite game of tricksters is the double-entendre. Odysseus uses the name "Udeis" which means "nobody," but also "hero," to trick Polyphemus the Cyclops. Cf. Max Horkheimer and Theodor W. Adorno, *Dialectic of Enlightenment*, trans. John Cumming (New York: Herder & Herder, 1972), p. 64. The tortoise in a Nigerian folktale takes the new name "All of You" at a feast, and gets the lion's share of the food prepared for "all of you." Cf. Chinua Achebe, *Things Fall Apart* (Ibadan, Nigeria: Heinemann Educational Books, 1972), pp. 87-88.

87 Joel Chandler Harris, introd. to *Uncle Remus: His Songs and His Sayings* (New York: D. Appleton-Century, 1947), p. xiv.

88 Joel Chandler Harris, *Brer Rabbit: Stories from Uncle Remus,* adapted by Margaret Wise Brown (New York: Harper Bros., 1971), p. 42. Similarly, in the Homeric Hymn to Hermes the Thief (who became identified with the lower-class struggle for equality with the aristocracy in sixth-century Athens), "references to Hermes as an inventor are frequent, vivid, and elaborate. In all of them, the individual and original genius of the inventor is emphasized." Cf. Norman O. Brown, *Hermes the Thief: The Evolution of a Myth* (Madison, Wisconsin: The University of Wisconsin Press, 1947), p. 75.

89 Karl Kerényi, in Paul Radin, *The Trickster: A Study in American Indian Mythology* (New York: Greenwood Press, 1969), p. 185.

90 Mauss has noted as an essential characteristic of magic and witchcraft that "most of the conditions which must be observed are abnormal ones. However commonplace, the magical rite has to be thought of as unique . . . all magical rites generally aim at endowing the ceremonies with an abnormal character. All movements are the opposite of normal ones, particularly those performed at religious ceremonies. Conditions, including those of time, are apparently unrealizable: materials are preferably unclean and the practices obscene. The whole thing is bizarre, involving artifice and unnatural features — very far removed from that simplicity to which recent theorists have wished to reduce magic." Cf. Marcel Mauss, *A General Theory of Magic,* trans. Robert Brain (London: Routledge & Kegan Paul, 1972), p. 50.

91 ". . . consider the distinctive appearance of prophets. They tend to arise in peripheral areas of society, and prophets tend to be shaggy, unkempt individuals. They express in their bodies the independence of social norms which their peripheral origins inspire in them. It is no accident that St. John the Baptist lived in the desert and wore skins, or that Nuer prophets wear beards and long hair in a fashion that ordinary Nuer find displeasing. Everywhere, social peripherality has the same physical forms of expression, bizarre and untrimmed." Cf. Mary Douglas, *Natural Symbols: Explorations in Cosmology* (New York: Vintage Books, 1973), p. 118.

92 *Ibid.,* p. 88.

93 Norman O. Brown, *Hermes the Thief,* p. 82.

94 When commercial classes in sixth-century Athens successfully challenged the ruling aristocracy and democratized political power, the cult of Hermes was ensconced alongside that of Apollo, "aristocrat of the gods," and at the same time Hermes' character was transformed, acquiring "the essential traits of the mythological type of culture hero, of which there is no finer example than the Greek Prometheus. Like Prometheus, Hermes is represented as 'pre-eminently in-

telligent' . . . . Like Prometheus again, Hermes is represented as a friend of mankind, a source of material blessings, 'the giver of good things,' 'the giver of joy.' " (*Ibid.*, p. 21). But the transformation of trickster into hero is not the only possibility. Peacock reports an example of mass-culture co-option occurring in contemporary, urban Java, where transvestites, closely related to the figure of the trickster, provide nightly stage entertainment for proletarian audiences, singing songs which transform traditional cultural meanings in a way that makes cultural sense out of new industrial conditions, functioning to justify the inequities of those conditions, rather than critically illuminating them. Cf. James L. Peacock, "Javanese Clown and Transvestite Songs: Some Relations between 'Primitive Classification' and 'Communicative Events,' " in *Essays on the Verbal and Visual Arts*, ed. June Helm (Seattle: University of Washington Press, 1967), pp. 64-76.

95 Jürgen Habermas, *Legitimation Crisis*, trans. Thomas McCarthy (Boston: Beacon Press, 1975).

96 Theodor W. Adorno, "Notizen zur neuen Anthropologie," Frankfurt am Main, Adorno Estate, 1942, p. 2.

97 Iggeret Magen Abraham (1668), cited in Gershom Scholem, *The Messianic Idea in Judaism* (New York: Schocken Books, 1971), p. 72.

98 Georg Lukács, *History and Class Consciousness*, p. 262.

99 G.W.F. Hegel, *The Phenomenology of Mind*, trans. J.B. Baillie (New York: Harper & Row, 1967), pp. 228-40.

100 Cf. Walter Benjamin, "The Author as Producer," *Understanding Brecht*, trans. Anna Bostock, (London: NLB, 1973), p. 86.

101 Jean Piaget, *Play, Dreams and Imitation in Childhood*, p. 73.

102 G. W. F. Hegel, *The Phenomenology of Mind*, p. 136.

103 Norman O. Brown, *Hermes the Thief*, pp. 83-86. Thus in the Hymn to Hermes, the latter urges Zeus to "uphold the cause of the young and the helpless." (Cited in *Ibid.*, p. 85).

104 This is the clear conclusion of empirical research cited in Ali Wacker (ed.), *Die Entwicklung des Gesellschaftsverständnises bei Kindern* (Frankfurt am Main: Campus Verlag, 1976), p. 47 and *passim*.

105 Michel Butor, "On Fairy Tales," trans. Remy Hall, *European Literary Theory and Practice: From Existential Phenomenology to Structuralism*, ed. Vernon Gras

(New York: Delta, 1973), pp. 352-354.

106 *Ibid.*, p. 352.

107 *Ibid.*, p. 356.

108 Philippe Ariès, *Centuries of Childhood: A Social History of Family Life,* trans. Robert Baldick (New York: Vintage Books, 1962). Not until the late seventeenth century did "fairy tales" as a distinct genre of children's literature begin to develop. It is important for our purposes to note that story-telling as a game common to all ages and all classes "was destroyed at one and the same time between children and adults, between lower class and middle class. This coincidence enables us to glimpse already a connection between the idea of childhood and the idea of class." (*Ibid.*, p. 99.)

109 For a discussion of the adult-child distinction in Tudor England corroborating Ariès' argument, and of the metaphorical parallels which were then drawn between adult-child structures and social structures threatened by civil war, see Boyd M. Berry, "The First English Pediatricians and Tudor Attitudes Toward Childhood," *Journal of the History of Ideas* 35 (October-December, 1974): 561-577.

110 "A world inverted, an exemplary world, fairyland is a criticism of ossified reality. It does not remain side by side with the latter; it reacts upon it, it suggests that we transform it, that we reinstate what is out of place." (Michel Butor, "On Fairy Tales," *European Literary Theory and Practice,* p. 353.)

111 *Ibid.*, p. 356. It should be pointed out that the dependency which results from certain *natural* characteristics, such as sex and race, has *social* origins, and is not surmounted by growing to adulthood: "whereas the difference between parents and children can be diminished, that between the sexes is accentuated." (*Ibid.*, p. 360.)

112 The constellations are, I believe, various but not limitless, as their structure would become visible in the arrangement of a handful of key elements. To outline a socio-historical, natural-historical typology of the ways in which social class and chronological age intersect in relation to domination (no doubt the variables of sex and race would also be crucial) would be a continuation of Adorno's own work in character typology, in *The Authoritarian Personality* (New York: Harper & Brothers, 1950), which in turn built on the work of Erich Fromm and other colleagues at the *Institut für Sozialforschung* (see that Institute's 1936 publication, *Autorität und Familie*). Here, by way of illustration, we might suggest several possibilities of types: (1) Upper-class child grows to membership in the ruling class, identifies helplessness with childishness, takes a paternal interest in the poor as a "Limousine Liberal;" (2) Upper-class child feels inferiority, feels as an adult he cannot fill his father's shoes, identifies with the poor because they are weak, becomes a

guilt-ridden radical with a politics of non-violent resistance; (3) Lower-middle-class child becomes socially marginal adult, fears recurrence of childhood impotence (fears being *overpowered* by his own *helplessness*), fears and is prejudiced against the poor and socially outcast, is attracted to a fascism; (4) Working-class child submits to parental authority, which he translates into social authority, accepts social impotency and gets recognition as a conscientious worker in return; represses his own power drives and deflects them onto family relations, becomes an authoritarian father, and the pattern repeats itself in the next generation; (5) Working-class child rebels against socially impotent parents but submits to social constraints in order to join upper class; and (6) Working-class child becomes autonomous adult, cannot reconcile adult potency with social impotency, comes into conflict with social authority. Particularly interesting regarding the fusing of natural and social experiences of impotency is recent work in the psycho-social interpretation of dreams. (I. T. Millán, *Mr. Mexico, Caracter e Ideologia del Ejecutivo Mexicano*, in preparation.)

113   Cf. Claude Lévi-Strauss, "The Structural Study of Myth," in *Structural Anthropology*, trans. Claire Jacobson and Brooke Grundfest Schoepf (New York: Basic Books, 1963), and Lévi-Strauss, "History and Dialectic," in *The Savage Mind* (Chicago: University of Chicago Press, 1973).

114 Jean Piaget, *Play, Dreams and Imitation in Childhood*, p. 149.

115 Kurt Vonnegut, Jr., *Cat's Cradle* (New York: Delacorte Press, 1963), pp. 134-145.

116 Theodor W. Adorno, *Negative Dialectics*, pp. 10-11.

Discussion

Hans Furth: Does Piaget's theory claim to be universal? Have you found a passage in Piaget's texts where Piaget indicates that others can make use of his theory? Of course Piaget isn't responsible for uses people make of his theory.

Susan Buck-Morss: Piaget is definitely a believer in science. He defines science as something that is universally applicable.

Furth: Do you project the label of "scientist" on him?

Buck-Morss: That's right. He is very excited by the idea that this should apply cross-culturally.

Furth: I don't think so. We know that there are different ways of formalizing things, and Piaget is not at all surprised that different results are found. I mentioned that he is very partial to formal thinking for precisely that reason. He is not sure whether formal thinking is a specialization of our Western culture or whether it is something that is found everywhere.

Buck-Morss: Yes, but that misses the point. Cultural relativists claim that this depends upon Western culture. I'm trying to say that the distinction between whether a Piagetian test is culturally relative or whether it affects a socio-economic structure is crucial. He admits to cultural relativity, but not to this reflection of socio-economic structure.

Furth: There is no Piagetian test in the sense that we use the word "test." Piaget never claimed to have any test.

Buck-Morss: That is a very important point. One of the really revolutionary, paradigm-breaking elements in Piaget's contributions to science is the fact that instead of doing tests over hundreds and thousands of people, he took three children—his own—and built the whole theory out of what any mother could do. This is the real beauty of it. You are right; this is a problem because, in order to make it verifiable, we have transformed it back into the old paradigm of science by quantitatively testing people cross-culturally.

Furth: You said that misses the point. What is the point? Let's say there are Piagetian tests, and Piaget could extend them to every culture. You would find a majority of people using our measurements who show some evidence of concrete operations and a minority of people who show some evidence of formal operations. That's what we see in our culture.

Buck-Morss: Adults act on something. The important factor is not this but that the amount of clay remains constant, and that it is based on a notion of mathematics or abstract equivalency. That is the point. It is not an issue of cultural relativism. Two plus two equals four everywhere. But in barter in Africa, concrete things are exchanged. On the other hand, the structure of our social and economic system is based on abstract exchange. That is what Marx wrote three volumes of *Capital* about. To give an example, a Ghanaian psychologist was doing a study of the conservation of clay among children of pottery makers. (The same amount of clay is shaped in different ways). Those children score higher on these tests than their non-pottery-making neighbors and than other children. In Western society, it has no connection with whether these people are potters' children or whether their parents ever pounded bread. It makes no difference because somehow or other it gets inculcated into the child that the important element is abstract equivalency no matter what else is happening in the procedure.

Furth: In our Western culture?

Buck-Morss: Luria, the Soviet psychologist, has studied the cognitive development of children during the period of the socialization of the farms in the 1930s. He finds that peasant villages, which are face to face to face societies based on locally consumed agricultural production, did not think abstractly, but when they are hooked up (in the same Russian culture) with a national abstract economy—here I am making no distinction between the West and the East—they indeed develop abstract cognition.

John Rajchman: I agree with you that there is a political input to the work of Piaget. I am thinking also of Michel Foucault and the questions he asks about how an object comes to be constituted, its genealogy and so on. In the case of Piaget, it seems to me that childhood itself should become an object of intelligence tests, that childhood is something which itself has to be examined. It is not clear that that examination can be reduced to the simple schema of reflection. You also mentioned the separation of form and content. Why does someone observe his daughter asking these particular questions? Why these questions about children? You said that Piaget uses Kantian schemes, but Kant himself did not apply these schemes to children. There may be a positive role to the knowledge which surrounds the child in the very reflection of the child. When a child is born now, the parents, for example, know a good deal about intelligence testing. When the child goes to school, tests are used. But the test may be a function of segregation. Do you think that this other kind of analysis would consider how childhood is constituted?

Buck-Morss: Adorno says that the experience of decentering your gaze is what is important. Every time you do something, you take pieces of existing schemes and put them together in new ways. Essentially any kind of text is a rewriting.

Rajchman: Let me put my question another way. It seems to me that one of the things that is important about developmental theory, especially abnormal and normal developmental theory, is positive dialectical theory of the child's cognition. Unlike Piaget, you introduce Adorno's negative dialectical theory of the sciences. But you arrive at a kind of absurd position when you are forced to ask whether there is normal and abnormal dialectical development.

Buck-Morss: You are right. One would have to redefine a lot of things. Otherwise, you would be in an absurd position.

Dick Howard: Let me agree with the political. Yet there is another

political question that needs to be raised. Charles Scott last night was trying to talk about historicity . . . missing elements and so on. I would ask
you though: is there any history in this negative dialectic? My question
would be: is the negative dialectic ahistorical and merely experiential? In
which case, it seems to me that it deals with what Charles Scott wanted,
but it doesn't deal with what you want. If not, how can you come up with
some sort of theory of development which would also be capable of dealing
with historical and revolutionary development?

Buck-Morss: Adorno has no theory of history. He couldn't have a theory
of history. That would be to posit one. You have to talk more about the
concept of time. He is very close to Freud. It was not accidental that he did
a dissertation on Freud in 1926-1927 just before converting to Marx. He
assumes that we are *in* the dialectic. We can not get out of the stream and
look at it as Engels tried to do by talking undialectically about the dialectic. What do you do from the fact that truth is relative to historical
time? Adorno states in a 1937 unpublished text that he was never bothered
by the problem of relativism. He found that the historical relativity of
truth does not rob one of the ability to make truthful judgments. It
demands that you do so. The truth of Piaget is the historical specificity of
his theory. Children do perform better in capitalist societies. The theory is
simply not universal and ahistorical. Once you give up the idea that any
kind of statement has to be eternally true and you accept the relativity of
truth, you have no more problem than Einstein does in saying that there is
only one right answer—given this point in time and space with this particular object. So given 1977 at this moment and place, there is a correct
answer. It is not an answer that I can hold and can give back to you a year
from now. That would be to reify. However, I can give it back to you a year
from now if the structure has not changed and hence it still has validity.
Not everything is in total flux. The world is not a grand Bergsonian chaos.
That is the way Adorno gets out of that problem. I found it convincing. It
does not bother me either.

Bernard Flynn: What you say leads to an apparent contradiction. On
the one hand, when you talk about Adorno and his notion of non-identity
or decentralization and when you make the critique of Piaget, you find in
the very structures not only of his test or his theory but of the reality of
childhood, the exact same structure that one finds in capitalist economy:
the equivalence, the exchange, the formalism, the abstract labor and so
on. Can you do this without a philosophy of identity? It seems to me to
make sense to do this from the perspective of Lukács, where the entire
culture is structured in terms of the same form. But can you maintain that

argument after rejecting the philosophy of identity?

Buck-Morss: I think you can, because what Adorno is saying about social theory is close to Erich Fromm — but Erich Fromm sets up theories in such a way that they do not contradict each other. Adorno maintains a contradiction. And that was a point that I tried to make. There is no "this is it; now you've got it," because if I am looking at psychological phenomena, I will tell you about society. As soon as you give me "Society" as the topic of my essay, I will tell you about psychology. Adorno does it every time. If you are talking about history, he will say "nature." If you are talking about nature, he will say "history." When you think that you have gotten around him by setting up a theory about something, he will just slide the ground from under you. It makes negative dialectics *negative* as opposed to Lukácsian. I mentioned that he studied music under Schönberg. In bourgeois tonal music, one note dominates — the dominant note. Atonality makes each note equally important. No note is more important than any other note. It seems to me that each of Adorno's essays has a similar structure, but in another, verbal mode. There is the element of the magician. He imagined Benjamin in a three-cornered hat. It fits Adorno as well. The role of the trickster is not unrelated except that the socially accepted trickster somehow always puts things back in order, whereas Adorno tries to shift that center. That may lead us to an understanding of the kind of diachronic development which Piaget, who is more concerned with synchronic stability, does not address. Piaget has more difficulty with diachronic development, which would imply that diachronic development involves a critical non-biological function, and one which still has very much to do with subject/object relationships.

Lloyd Zamchuk: How is the scientific goal to be separated from a dialectical goal?

Buck-Morss: The distinction was not between scientific and dialectic. The distinction was between whether we want someone to be critical in the scientific sense, which means not accepting the conception of reality, but rather seeing for oneself — holding, tasting, touching, feeling, doing one's own experiments on it — the kind of critical desire to see for oneself that Piaget was talking about in the quotation that I read. That is what I would mean by critical in a scientific sense. The world of a social critic is a very different one. For instance, when is Joan of Arc a witch and when is she a visionary? When is Jesus a magician and when is he a miracle-worker? That involves the control of the production of meanings. I mean there are always witches and as long as they accept themselves as witches, as many who confess at trials do, as long as the people on the periphery (a kind of counter-hegemony) accept the peripheral world, they are okay. However, when they try to say that they are not witches, but that they are visionaries, they begin to throw things off center — they become socially dangerous.

Furth: I do not like the role of saying what Piaget means, but I find that I am trying to adapt Piaget's thinking to your thinking and what we include in thinking is precisely what you are saying. We show our children what that should be. We expose them to the fact that any intelligence is merely what is culturally expected. There is not one right answer to any factor. There are different perspectives.

Buck-Morss: I would disagree with you. What you are teaching them is wrong. I think that there is one right answer. Again the dichotomy is not between relativism on the one hand and absolute science on the other. The distinction is between relativism and relativity, which I tried to make in the case of history.

Furth: It is impossible not to be political. Of course, Piaget is political. Skinner is political. Adorno is political. We are all political. We would be idiots to think that, in our culture, we can exist outside of politics. Piaget has endeavored to show that cognition is part and parcel of every human behavior. If Piaget posits this cognition, it must lead to dialectical revolution. The very notion of thinking of the possibility of thinking alternatives implies going beyond the present. If Piaget has done anything, he has pointed out that there is no absolute beginning and no absolute end.

Buck-Morss: One distinction which is not clear here is the distinction between positive and negative dialectics.

Harvey Gross: I was interested in what you said, almost as an aside, that Adorno did not have a theory of history. Yet I am also thinking of what you said, or what Adorno has said, about the development of atonal music, namely that the development of atonality was inevitable and that it was already determined perhaps in Beethoven's second period. There is or seems to be a determinism in the way Adorno thinks. He makes it absolutely clear that atonality is a logical necessity that develops out of tonality. Secondly, Adorno is fascinated with Spengler and his notions of decadence. On what basis do you say that there is no theory of history?

Buck-Morss: Let's take your last point first. His fascination with Spengler. This is a perfect example of the decentering that I'm talking about. Adorno was never fascinated with Spengler until after 1940 when he read Benjamin's thesis that nothing has corrupted the working class so much as the sense that it was moving with the current. The whole notion of progress in history has been lethal because Hitler caught the wave of history. Then everybody charged on. At this point, because of the present reality—not as an ontological theory of history—it is now urgently compelling to brush history against the grain. Benjamin wrote that for Marx revolutions are the locomotives of history, which we have to redefine as humanity reaching for the emergency brake. What they said about history and what they said about progress in 1929 was favorable, because then a static view of reality was retrogressive. Later they struggled against the notion of progress—with Hitler as the man of history.

Gross: Whether you believe in a theory of progress or a theory of decadence, you still have a theory of history.

Buck-Morss: No. No. They believed in neither/nor. Adorno believed that it was absolutely necessary to keep consciousness critical, which meant essentially to oppose whatever may have been the ruling view. You can accuse him of being a non-conformist, an anarchist, a Nietzschean, but not a Spenglerian.

PIAGET, LACAN, AND LANGUAGE

William J. Richardson

Piaget's reaction to the work of Jacques Lacan is par for the course. "No matter what the outcome," he writes, "the project in itself is of great interest. But not until the 'uninitiated' have 'clarified' Lacan's results will we be in a position to gauge their value."[1] In other words, Lacan seems to have something good to say, if only we could understand it. It is reassuring to learn that even for the perspicacious mind of a Piaget, Lacan's exposition leaves something to be desired.

The remark occurs in Piaget's book, *Structuralism,* where, after explaining his own conception of structure as a "self-regulating, transformational totality,"[2] he reviews the principal forms of structuralism in the various physical and social sciences, listing Lacan under the etiquette of "linguistic" structuralism and describing his effort as follows:

> . . . All psychoanalysis, [Lacan] points out, has speech for its medium; that of the analyst, who normally says very little, but chiefly the speech of the patient; indeed, the psychoanalytic process consists essentially of the patient's "translating" his unconscious individual symbols into a conscious and public language. Taking off from this new idea, Lacan has tried to use linguistic structuralism and familiar mathematical models to devise new transformation rules which would make it possible for the irrational ingredients of the unconscious and the ineffable features of private symbols to make their entry into a language really designed to express the communicable.[3]

The wording here is suggestive and worth comment, but let us be content for the moment with finding in this passage an indication in bold strokes of what profoundly differentiates the two men as well as what unites them in common interest. Piaget is a genetic epistemologist, Lacan a psychoanalyst; the former concerned chiefly with the qualitative development of the structures of individual knowing and thinking (i.e., of the rational, conscious processes of the self), the latter concerned with the structures of human desiring (i.e., with the irrational, unconscious dimensions of the self). What unites them is the common concern for structure and the recognition (though much more radically in Lacan) of the significant role of language in human development. It would be silly to minimize the differences, and even sillier to try to establish a cheap concordism between them. This would trivialize them both. What I propose here is to note the place where their paths seem to cross and ask if there is any way to think beyond it.

What I have in mind is that both pay very special attention to the moment when words first begin to be formed by the child. Piaget recalls how at about the age of sixteen months his little daughter slid a shell along a box saying "meow" just after seeing a cat on a wall;[4] Lacan, for his part, recalls the incident recounted by Freud of how a child who was "not at all precocious in his intellectual development" threw a wooden reel over the edge of his bed, then retrieved it while uttering the sounds of "oh-ah".[5] The incidents themselves are quite similar: in each case the child is using the inchoation of articulated speech to somehow make present an "object" (in one case a cat, in the other the mother) that is absent. How, then, does Piaget's analysis of this event differ from Lacan's?

For the genetic epistemologist, this incident is an example of the emergence of what he calls the "symbolic function" in the child. This occurs at the end of the sensori-motor stage of development, beginning at about the age of eighteen months. Up to that time the infant has shown a kind of practical intelligence aimed at solving problems; of action (for example, reaching distant or hidden objects), but these solutions are essentially a series of perceptions and movements, hence a partial coordination of actions that is sensori-motor in nature. During this period the child deals continually with signifiers (i.e., indicators/signals of one kind or another), but these signals are always perceptual and, though in each case they refer to something, are undifferentiated from what they refer to (for example, the visible part of a half-hidden toy is not differentiated from the whole).[6] But now behavior patterns develop in which the signifier begins to be distinct (i.e., differentiated) from what is signified so that the signifier represents the signified in various ways that Piaget enumerates as follows: (1) deferred imitation (i.e., imitation that starts after the disappearance of the model for it, for example the little girl who, after seeing a playmate become angry, scream, and stamp her foot, imitates the playmate later on, laughing); (2) symbolic play, (i.e., make-believe, for example this same girl pretending to sleep—sitting down and smiling but closing her eyes, hand on one side, thumb in mouth, holding the corner of the tablecloth and pretending it is the corner of the pillow); (3) drawing or graphic images; (4) the internalizing of an imitation of the signified in the form of a mental image; finally (5) the vocal evocation of an event that is not occurring at that time (for example, the "meow" that represents the absent cat, or the "Anpa bye-bye" that translates into "Grandpa has gone away".[7]

Now all of these forms of rendering present what is absent (i.e., representation) may be considered specimens of intellectual actions for Piaget, even nascent forms of thought as he uses the word, wherein signifiers are differentiated from what they signify, but only the last of them may be called in any formal way "speech." Hence, speech is only a late-developing part of the symbolic function, understood now as the capacity to represent reality through the intermediary of signifiers that are distinct from what they signify.

Clearly, then, representative thought for Piaget does not begin with and result from the incorporation of verbal signs from the social environment. It is not the acquisition of speech that gives rise to the symbolic function, but rather the symbolic function precedes and makes way for the acquisition of speech. Initially, the first differentiated signifiers have the property of private, idiosyncratic symbols rather than of social signs—symbols that do not articulate a name but rather express an appeal or desire for a presence. Eventually, of course, these social signs, systematized into a linguistic code that is commonly shared with other subjects, play an essential role in the development of conceptual thinking.

The precise relationship between the individual child's nascent capacity for speech and the broader parameters of language as a social institution and code (between ontogenesis and phylogenesis, as Piaget puts it)[8] is a problem that engages the whole issue of his conception of structure. He admits readily that the child's capacity for speech cannot be measured by what he learns from experience alone and thereby rejects a logical positivist, strictly empiricist view of language development (for example, Bloomfield), yet he cannot accept the contrary view of Noam Chomsky that there is in every human being a fixed innate schema of reason according to which the grammar of a natural language is developed by certain rules of transformation out of the "kernel sentences" of an elemental, "generative" grammar.[9] Instead, he argues for what he calls a "constructive" view of speech development that parallels his conception of the way intelligence and thought develop.

Since his earliest beginnings as a biologist, Piaget's model for human growth was that of a biological organism interacting with its environment. "The image of an active organism which both selects and incorporates stimuli in a manner determined by its structure, while at the same time adapting its structure to the stimuli, emerged from these early studies as a ready-made model for cognitive development."[10] Accordingly, what characterizes intelligence is a set of functional characteristics that perdure rather than inborn structural limitations which in fact change and are replaced over time. The basic functional characteristics of this adaptational process are assimilation and accommodation: assimilating the new to the old and accommodating the old to the new. By this dialectical self-adaptive process, the self maintains its equilibrium in the environment, hence it is sometimes called a process of "equilibration." If such a model is applied to the development of speech in the child, does it suffice to explain his relationship to language as a social institution? That is a critical question, and we shall have to return to it. For the moment, let it suffice to say that the little self who says "meow" has assimilated these sounds from her language environment and accommodates to her loss by the function of imitation that lets an absence become present through inchoative speech.

Lacan's reflection on the "oh-ah" experience is based upon the famous anecdote reported in "Beyond the Pleasure Principle":

> This good little boy had an occasional disturbing habit of taking any small objects he could get hold of and throwing them away from him into a corner, under the bed, and so on, so that hunting for his toys and picking them up was often quite a business. As he did this he gave vent to a loud, long drawn-out "o-o-o-o," accompanied by an expression of interest and satisfaction. His mother and the writer of the present account were agreed in thinking that this was not a mere interjection but represented the German word *Fort* ["gone"]. I eventually realized that it was a game and that the only use he made of any of his toys was to play "gone" with them. One day I made an observation which confirmed my view. The child had a wooden reel with a piece of string tied round it. It never occurred to him to pull it along the floor behind him, for instance, and play at its being a carriage. What he did was to hold the reel by the string and very skillfully throw it over the edge of his curtained cot, so that it disappeared into it, at the same time uttering his expressive "o-o-o-o." He then pulled the reel out of the cot again by the string and hailed its reappearance with a joyful *"Da!"* ["there"]. This, then, was the complete game — disappearance and return.[11]

For Freud, the meaning of the game was obvious. "It was related to the child's great cultural achievement—the instinctual renunciation (i.e., the renunciation of instinctual satisfaction) which he had made in allowing his mother to go away without protesting . . . . " (p. 15). For Lacan, the "cultural achievement" here does not consist simply in the child's "renunciation of instinctual satisfaction" but rather in his experience of desire for her precisely in separating from her and in dealing with this frustrated desire through the little game of which inchoatively verbal sounds were an essential part. In Lacan's words, the moment "in which desire becomes human is also that in which the child is born into language."[12]

How precisely is the child at this point "born into language?" Lacan's own enigmatic answer is as follows:

> [The child's action], immediately taking body in the symbolic couple of two elementary jaculations, announces in the subject the . . . integration of the dichotomy of the phonemes, whose . . . structure existing language offers to his assimilation; moreover, the child begins to become engaged in the system of concrete discourse of the environment, by reproducing more or less approximately in his *Fort!* and in his *"Da!"* the vocables which he receives from it.[12]

But that needs a little bit of unpacking.

Lacan, we know, is first of all a psychoanalyst. The essentials of his position can be simply stated: he wants to reread Freud—radically! According to him, the greatness of Freud's discovery consisted in the fact that it was an insight into the import of the "talking" cure. Scientifically trained, however, Freud wanted to make his insights scientifically respectable, but the only scientific model available to him at the time was that of nineteenth century physics. In our own day, we have available another scientific model (a more characteristically human one) for understanding the psyche: the science of linguistics—a science that explores the structures discernible in the one phenomenon that is coextensive with man himself (i.e., human language). Linguistics has already thrown light on other disciplines, particularly anthropology (for example, the work of Sapir and Whorf in America, Lévi-Strauss in Europe) and Lacan's intention is to let it now throw light on psychoanalysis.

To appreciate what the structuralists see in linguistics that leads them to take it as a paradigm for their work, recall for a moment Lévi-Strauss' explanation:

Among all social phenomena language alone has thus far been studied
in a manner which permits it to serve as the object of truly scientific
analysis, allowing us to understand its formative process and to predict its
mode of change. This results from modern researches into the problems
of phonemics, which have reached beyond the superficial conscious and
historical expression of linguistic phenomena to obtain fundamental and
objective realities consisting of systems of relations which are the products
of unconscious thought processes. The question which now arises is this: is
it possible to effect a similar reduction in the analysis of other forms of
social phenomena? If so, would this analysis lead to the same result? And
if the answer to this last question is in the affirmative, can we conclude
that all forms of social life are substantially of the same nature—that is,
do they consist of systems of behavior that represent the projection, on the
level of conscious and socialized thought, of universal laws which regulate
the unconscious activities of the mind?[13]

The answer for Lévi-Strauss is "Yes."

It is "Yes" for Lacan too. His task becomes, then, to explore the "universal laws" that regulate the "unconscious activities" of the mind, where
these "universal laws" are the laws of language and the "unconscious activities" are those processes that Freud discovered and which he designated
simply as "the unconscious." We may assume, I think, that we all have
some notion of what Freud meant by "the unconscious." What is meant
here by the "universal laws" of language? We know well enough that since
Saussure in modern times language has been considered a system of signs,
and that these signs are composed of a relationship between a signifying
component (a sound image) and a signified component (a concept), the
relationship itself being arbitrary (i.e., nonnecessary; for example, there is
no necessary connection between the word "horse" and our four-footed
friends—*cheval, Pferd, equus* will do as well). In one of his essays Lacan
speaks of these signifiers as composed of "ultimate distinctive features" that
are the phonemes (i.e., the smallest distinctive group of speech sounds in
any language). These signifiers in turn are combined according to the
"laws of a closed order," (i.e., laws of vocabulary and of grammar according to which phonemes are grouped into units of meaning of increasing complexity, such as words, phrases, clauses, sentences, etc.)[14]

The elementary particles of language, therefore, are the phonemes.
Jakobson and Halle have made an exhaustive study of these phonemes and
discovered that all possible sounds may be divided according to a system of
bi-polar opposition into twelve sets of binary pairs "out of which each
language makes its own selection."[15] When Lacan sees in the *Fort-Da* experience, then, an articulation "taking body in the symbolic couple of two

elementary jaculations, it announces in the subject the . . . integration of the dichotomy of the phonemes, whose . . . structure existing language offers to his assimilation,"[16] he seems to be saying that in this primitive fashion the child first experiences the bi-polar nature of the ultimate rudiments of language, the phonemes. "From this pair [of sounds] modulated on presence and absence . . . there is born a particular language's universe of sense in which the universe of things will come into line"[17] (i.e., become present in their absence).

Now the units of meaning composed out of phonemes (words, phrases, clauses, etc.) relate to one another along one or other of two fundamental axes of language: an axis of combination and an axis of selection. Here again the pioneer work was done by Roman Jakobson.[18] Along the axis of combination, linguistic units are related to one another insofar as they are co-present to each other. Thus the words that I am using now in this very sentence, even though stretched out in a linear sequence that suspends their full meaning to the end, are related to each other by a type of co-presence (i.e., they are connected to each other by a certain contiguity in time). The second axis along which linguistic units relate to each other, however, is an axis of selection. This means that they do not relate to each other by reason of a co-presence but rather by some kind of mutual exclusion, whether this is because one word is chosen over another as being more appropriate (for example, we speak of Lacan as a "structuralist" rather than as a "physician") or because one word implies the rejection of its antonym (for example, by calling him a "structuralist," we imply that he is not an "existentialist," etc.). Thus, to select one unit is to exclude the other, but at the same time the excluded other is still available to be substituted for the first if circumstances warrant. The axis of selection, then, is also an axis of possible substitution.

These two principles of combination and selection permeate the entire structure of language. Thus, Jakobson was able to analyze the nature of aphasia according to whether the patient was deficient in terms of the axis of combination or the axis of selection.[19] Now, when these two axes of combination and selection function in terms of the relationship between signifiers, we find that signifiers either may be related to each other by a principle of combination (i.e., in terms of some kind of contiguity with each other (for example, a relationship of cause/effect, part/whole, sign/thing signified, etc.), in other words, by reason of what the old rhetoric of Quintilian called "metonymy;" or they may be related by a principle of selection (i.e., in virtue of the fact that one is substituted for the other — in other words, by "metaphor.") For example, on the morning

following the first Nixon-Frost interview, a radio news headline announc-
ed: "Nixon discusses Watergate affair; Australia has its own Watergate."
In each case, "Watergate" is used to signify a political scandal: in the first
case, it does so by contiguity (i.e., by designating the place where a
political scandal first began to be uncovered, hence by metonymy); in the
second case, it does so by substitution (i.e., the word "Watergate,"
already clothed in metonymic associations, is used to substitute for the term
"political scandal," hence by metaphor). If we say, then, that signifiers are
related to each other under the guise of either metonymy or metahor, this
is simply to transpose the laws of combination and selection into another
key. Let this suffice, then, to indicate the sort of thing that is meant when
we speak here of "the laws of language."

But how do these relate to the nature of the unconscious as Freud experienced it? It is Lacan's thesis that Freud's insight into the nature of the
talking cure was an insight into the way the laws of language work in a
relationship between signifiers that may be described as either metonymy
or metaphor. Thus, when he analyzes the workings of the unconscious in
the form of the dream work that elaborates the essential message of the
dream by distortions, Lacan sees here at work the linguistic laws of combination and substitution. For when Freud speaks of "condensation,"
Lacan understands this as essentially a substitution (i.e., a metaphor), and
when Freud speaks of "displacement," Lacan understands this as combination by contiguity (i.e., metonymy). It is correlations such as these that
permit Lacan to say that the unconscious is structured like a language.[20] [21]

Let us return to the child's game of *Fort-Da,* the moment when he is
"born into language." To do justice to the complexity of Lacan's thought
at this point, we should not forget that it is also the moment in which
"desire becomes human" and that the vagaries of desire as it erupts in the
moment of separation from the mother are intimately associated with the
burgeoning power of speech in the child. For the sake of simplicity,
however, we restrict our attention to the issue of speech.

That the child has the capacity to stimulate the *Fort-Da* with his "oh"
and "ah" is a matter of native equipment. That at this point he begins to
exercise it is a matter of maturation. As Lacan puts it, "the child begins to
become engaged in the system of the concrete discourse of the environment, by reproducing more or less approximately in his '*Fort!*' and in his
'*Da!*' the vocables which he receives from it."[22] Let us note then: that given
a matrix of possible phonemes, it is the environment of the natural
language that determines which ones are assimislated by the child; that the
pair that is assimilated expresses the experience of presence through

absence; that what characterizes this moment for Lacan is the fact that although the natural language has surrounded the child from the beginning of life, it is only now that the child actively begins to make the language his own.

But how the child passes from this moment of incipient speech into the domain of language as a social institution is for Lacan more than a matter of self-regulating equilibration. He sees here a profound evolution from a dyadic relationship with the mother into a profoundly pluralized relationship to society as a whole. The father, then, is more than the third member of the Oedipal triangle—he is the symbol and representative of the social order as such into which the child by the acquisition of speech now enters. The social order is governed by a set of relationships that govern all forms of human interchange (for example, the forming of pacts, gift-giving, marriage ties, kinship relations, etc.). This mapping of human relationship with its symbolic arrangements Lacan speaks of as "law," to suggest, I suppose, the patterning, compelling quality of it. It any case, this law is characteristically human, for, Lacan writes, ". . . in regulating marriage ties [it] superimposes the kingdom of culture on that of nature abandoned to the law of copulation. The interdiction of incest is only its subjective pivot . . . . "[23] This law is what Lévi-Strauss has called the "symbolic order," an order of signs designating the primordial arrangement of society. Lacan, following Lévi-Strauss here,[24] finds that this primordial law that sets the pattern for human relationships is the same law that sets the pattern of human language. "The law of man has been the law of language," he writes, "since the first words of recognition presided over the first gifts."[25]

In any case, the symbolic order represented by the father is the field, or domain, in which the child becomes an active citizen when he acquires the power of speech. The essence of Freud's discovery, Lacan claims, was to see the relationship between the individual psyche and the symbolic order in terms of man's unconscious dimension. "Isn't it striking," he writes, "that Lévi-Strauss, in suggesting the implication of the structures of language with that part of the social laws which regulate marriage ties and kinship, is already conquering the very terrain in which Freud situates the unconscious."[26]

Let us regroup here. We are taking account of that place where Piaget and Lacan cross paths as both reflect on the moment of great mystery when the child begins to articulate sounds in order to let presence emerge out of absence. At this point, we can say that each of them conceives the problem of language differently. For if Saussure's distinction between language and speech is still valid — and I think it is — the distinction according to which language is conceived as a social institution (a code or system that dwells unconsciously in any given language community) and speech is the individual conscious act of one who uses the code to express himself, then Piaget's focus is on the genesis of speech rather than on language, and the "symbolic function" is something that comes to pass in every individual rather than in the social order as such. For Lacan, on the other hand, the concern is with language at least as much as with speech; the symbolic function, however it may operate in the individual, belongs first of all to the social order, and the special problem seems to be to determine how language, as the unconscious structure of the social order, permeates the functioning of individual acts of speech.

We could call this simply an accidental coincidence, perhaps, like two ships passing in the night, if Piaget did not offer us some tantalizing texts that invite us to take the matter further. To begin with, he would probably reject Lacan's notion of a "symbolic order," for he criticizes the same notion in Lévi-Strauss:

> This grand theory is saddled with one major problem, which is: once we have admitted the existence of structures as distinct from the system of observable relations and interactions . . . how are we to understand this "existence?" What does it consist in? Structures are not simply convenient theoretical constructs; they exist apart from the anthropologist, for they are the *source* of the relations he observes; a structure would lose all truth value if it did not have this direct connection with the facts. But neither are they transcendent essences, for Lévi-Strauss is not a phenomenologist . . . . The recurrent formula is that structures "emanate from the intellect," from the human mind as ever the same; this is why they are prior to, rather than, as Durkheim would have it, derivative from the social order; prior to the "mental" as well [as] . . . and, *a fortiori,* to the "organic" . . . . But what manner of existence is left, then, for the mind, if it is neither social, nor mental in the subjective sense, nor organic?[27]

In other words, if we take Lévi-Strauss/Lacan seriously, *where* is the symbolic order? Piaget's own answer is: nowhere other than in the collectivity of human selves. Each functions in interaction with his environment and is self-regulating (i.e., self-constructing, equilibration). "From this perspective, there is no longer any need to choose between the primacy of the social or that of the intellect; the collective intellect is the social equilibrium resulting from the interplay of the operations that enter into all cooperation. Nor does intelligence precede mental life or the reverse; it is the equilibrated form of all cognitive functions."[28]

But this is the biologist talking, still rooted in an organic conception of morphogenesis. In his later years, however, and especially in *Structuralism*, he also seems to be something more. For the rigor of his own method pushes him to the brink of a new kind of question, a specifically philosophical one, or at least a different kind of philosophical question than can be extrapolated from his own epistemology — as if to confirm the old platitude which says that any epistemology, no matter how scientific, when taken to its limits ends in ontology.

What I have in mind particularly is his notion of the epistemic subject. " . . . Structuralism," he writes, "calls for a differentiation between the *individual subject*, who does not enter at all, and the *epistemic subject*, that cognitive nucleus which is common to all subjects at the same level.'[29] But what for Piaget is the nature of this "epistemic subject?" Not something "impersonal and general" he tells us:

> It might seem that the foregoing account makes the *subject* disappear to leave only the "impersonal and general," but this is to forget that on the plane of knowledge . . . the subject's activity calls for the continual "de-centering" without which he cannot become free from his spontaneous intellectual egocentricity. This "de-centering" makes the subject enter upon, not so much an already available and therefore external universality, as an uninterrupted process of coordinating and setting [i.e., developing] reciprocal relations. It is the latter process which is the true "generator" of structures as constantly under construction and reconstruction. The subject exists because, to put it very briefly, the "being" of structures consists in their coming to be, i.e., their being "under construction" [*l'être des structures c'est leur structuration*].[30]

My claim is that there is more here than epistemology. I take Piaget to be saying that the quest for the structures of human knowing have led him to postulate the presence in the knower of a subjectivity beneath the level of individualized consciousness; that on this level the self is somehow decentered (i.e., de-ego-centered, yet still "the center of functional activity")[31]; that this de-centered center is the core of the structuration process — of the coming-to-be and passing-away of structures; and that this core is best described not as the "universal" subject (an abstraction) nor as a "transcendental" subject but as the "Being" of the subject, constituting his very existence.

Now there is a striking parallel to this notion of the de-centered

epistemic subject in Lacan. For him, the speaking subject is not a conscious ego, as that term is normally understood, for he conceives of the ego
as rather an objectified reflection of the true self and in that sense already
an alienation of this self. The genuine self has a double dimension—one
dimension according to which it can say "I" and institute a discourse with
another human subject, and another dimension according to which the
subject is exposed to the order of language and its laws, as if to another
subject within itself, ex-centric to its conscious self, to which the conscious
self is inextricably—yet unconsciously—related. This "other" dimension of
the subject is precisely what Freud called "the unconscious"—"its force,"
Lacan tells us, "comes from the truth and in the dimension of Being: *kern
unseres Wesens* are Freud's own terms."[21] This Being-dimension of the self
for Lacan is the ground for those experiences common to the Being of all
men such as are captured so often in myth,[33] the ground even for neurosis
in the sense that "a neurosis is a question which Being poses for a subject
'from the place where it was before the subject came into the world'
[Freud's phrase which he used in explaining the Oedipal complex to Little
Hans.]"[34]

How are we to understand Being here? Lacan answers: "The 'Being'
referred to is that which appears in a lightning moment in the void of the
word 'to be' and I said that it poses its question for the subject. What does
that mean? It does not pose it *before* the subject, since the subject cannot
come to the place where it is posed, but it poses it *in place of* the (*à la place
du*) subject, that is, in that place it poses the question *with* the subject, as
one poses a problem *with* a pen . . . ."[35] Does this sound like Heidegger?
Indeed it does, and Lacan explicitly admits the influence. In fact, at one
point in his career he personally translated into French and published an
essay of Heidegger—the essay on *Logos* in Heraclitus.[36] In any case, we
have reason to find in Heidegger some paradigm for Lacan's notion of an
ex-centric subject, and I want to suggest the hypothesis that it may help us
understand Piaget's epistemic subject too.

I realize, of course, that this involves a shift of method, more radical for
Piaget than for Lacan. It may not work, but I feel that the effort is
justified, since in this regard Piaget's own method has taken us as far as it
can go, leaving us with a problem that this method cannot explore. "Of
course," he writes, "human structures do not arise out of nothing . . . . So
there are certain givens from which the construction of logical structures
takes off, but these 'data' are not primordial in any absolute sense, being
merely the starting point for our analysis . . . ."[37] My suggestion is that if
we adopt a more candidly ontological method, we may reach a deeper

understanding of the "givens" with which Piaget's own work begins.

The method I am suggesting comes from phenomenology (i.e., from Heidegger). The basic parameters of his thought are familiar. It is commonplace knowledge now that in search of the meaning of Being (*Sein*), Heidegger chooses phenomenology as his method, and the phenomenon par excellence that he examines is man (i.e., *Dasein*), because man obviously has some vague awareness (*Seinsverständnis*) of what Being means inasmuch as he can and does speak, say "is." Heidegger begins the analysis by taking *Dasein* as he is found with other *Dasein*s in his everyday condition as Being-in-the-World. He first analyzes the meaning of World, then the nature of Being-*in*-the-World with its four existential components of *Verstehen* ("understanding"), *Befindlichkeit* ("state of mind"), *Rede* "discourse"), and *Verfallen* ("fallenness"). He then tries to see this complex being in its unity (*Sorge*: care) and in its totality (i.e., as defined by its ultimate limit [death]). After this, he explores the sources of this unified totality in the still deeper unity of time, with everything that this implies concerning historicity, history, and all that goes with it. All of this is well known. Let us simply focus our attention on a few themes that might help us situate the problem at issue here.

Let us begin with *Dasein*. *Dasein* is an ex-centric, de-centered self whose own Being consists in its openness to the Being of all beings (including itself—that mysterious process that lights up all beings from the inside and lets them present themselves to man as what they are. As such, *Dasein* can indeed relate to other beings as a conscious ego, for it can and does say "I"—this is called its "ontic" dimension. But it is more than a conscious ego—it transcends all beings to their very Being—this is called its "ontological" dimension.

But since the center of *Dasein*'s ontological movement is Being and Being is "other" than the beings that surround *Dasein* and form the lateral center of its day-to-day interaction, this self is genuinely de-centered, excentric. However, the Being to which it is exposed is the Being of beings it deals with every day. Hence, *Dasein* enjoys a native familiarity with them that enables it to interact with them on a level of intimacy far more profound than any relationship from knower to known. Because of its openness to Being *Dasein* is "at home" in its environment—it is basically a doer caught up in a dynamic interchange with things. In this sense, it is certainly a "center of functional activity."

This will become clearer if we consider one of the fundamental existential components of *Dasein* called *Verstehen*. I call it "component" to underline the fact that we are talking about a constituent element of a self that is essentially a movement—movement through beings toward Being. *Verstehen* is usually translated "understanding," but it is important to realize that Heidegger does not intend anything cerebral here, like abstract thought or discursive reasoning. Rather it is that component through which *Dasein's* disclosive power (*Seinsverständnis*) is executed (i.e., the power by which *Dasein* X-rays the Being-structure of the beings it deals with so as to be able to interact with them in terms of their innermost core). For this reason, *Verstehen*, though not as such intelligence, is the ontological basis for what on the ontic level we call "intellectual activity"—knowing, thinking, reasoning, etc.—from its most primitive to its most sophisticated form. This existential understanding of beings, then, would be the ontological base for the "givens" with which Piaget's work begins. Thus, what is ontologically a communion with beings of one's environment becomes discernible on the ontic level of scientific scrutiny as "a process of coordinating and [developing] reciprocal relations."[38] It is because *Dasein*, by virtue of its understanding, already discloses the interiority of beings that on the ontic level the "Being of [its] structures consists in their coming to be (i.e., their being "under construction).[39] It is thus that all equilibration (structuration, "dialectic") is possible.

The existential constitution of *Dasein* includes another component: *Rede*. Often translated "discourse," the German word itself translates for Heidegger the Greek word "*logos*," and I would like to translate it back into the Greek for a reason that will become clear in a moment. How are we to understand it? The *logos* is another dynamic component of *Dasein's* openness to Being within the World, rooted in *Dasein's* own Being just as deeply as *Verstehen*, whose specific function is to make possible the articulation in human speech of what *Dasein* through the component of understanding discloses. If such a conception is acceptable, several consequences will follow, but let us note only one. This radical grounding of the capacity for human speech would make it possible, perhaps, to account for the "innate" qualities of what Chomsky calls the "deep structures" of a generative grammar without resorting to his thorough-going rationalism to explain them. Piaget could say of Chomsky's generative grammar what he says of a theory of preformed logical structures:

> True, there will always be some to urge that all the "subject" does is to bring "virtual" structures which subsist from eternity together. . . . But as soon as he breaks beyond the confines of his expertise and tries to develop an epistemology, he will have to ask himself where, exactly, this region of the virtual is to be located. To call on essences to furnish the virtual with its underpinnings is to beg the question, nor can the physical world pro-

vide its habitation. It makes far better sense to assign the virtual a place in organic life, though obviously only on condition that it be clearly understood that general algebra is not "contained" in the behavior of bacteria or viruses. So what remains is, again, the constructivist hypothesis, and is it not quite plausible to think of the nature that underlies physical reality as constantly in process of construction rather than as a heap of finished structures?"

Certainly — as long as we are content to think that nature deeply enough (i.e., not in terms of an epistemology but of an ontology that explores the Being of that nature, with all that this implies for the Being of the epistemic subject).

Being — what is the nature of this Being to which *Dasein* is open? Initially it is discerned as the Being of beings encountered in the World, then as more than this — as the World itself, experienced as a matrix of relationships (Total Meaningfulness) interior to which these beings find a place and have a meaning. But this is the perspective of the early Heidegger, of *Being and Time*,[41] which took man for the starting point of the analysis. Later on the focus shifts, and Heidegger attempts to meditate the sense of Being by thinking it, so to speak, for itself. He returns to the early Greeks to meditate their ways of bringing their experience of Being to expression in words like *physis* (nature), *a-letheia* (truth), and, in Heraclitus, *logos.* Let us restrict our attention to the *logos* of Heraclitus. For the early Greeks, the word *logos* came from *legein,* meaning "to gather, collect, bring together, lay out in the open," etc. As *logos,* then, Being was experienced as a gathering process that collected all beings together within themselves and in relationship to one another.[42] Above all, it is a process that lets beings appear as what they are, a letting-them-lie-forth in all the freshness of their original presencing.

How, then, did such a term ever come to mean "speech" or "language?" Heidegger's claim is that speech, long before it became an instrument of communication, is that process in man by which he responds to, corresponds with, the gathering process (*logos*) in beings and through the functioning of the *logos* within himself lets *logos* lie forth in words. To name something properly, for example, is to call it forth, in the sense of laying it out in the open, in such a way that the being can shine forth as what it is. "The process of naming (*onoma*) is not the expressing of the meaning of a word but letting-something-lie-forth in that light wherein it takes its stand [as a being, simply] inasmuch as it has a name."[43] To speak in this way, of course, is the special privilege of the poet, but all other language is a derivation — or a degeneration — from this primordial experience.

The way from the conception of language as correspondence with the *logos* by calling beings into presence to the conception of language as a system of signs or code of communication is, of course, a long and winding road that we cannot follow here. For the moment, let us infer at least this much: an experience of Being-as-*logos*, the One that gathers the many unto themselves and lets them relate to one another, is an experience of language in its origins, of aboriginal Language. As such, it is also the source of the cohesiveness of all things that are, hence the principle of all order, and specifically the foundation for the symbolic order as such, the ontological base of language as social institution and code. If Jakobson in his researches discovers the laws of phonemes or the two great axes of language that Lacan then sees to be structuring the unconscious as it permeates man, then these are ontic modalities, discernible by scientific scrutiny, of the primordial *logos* as such. Primordial, it has a certain priority over man—that is why Lacan can speak of it as "wagging us," of "Language speaking man" rather than the reverse.

Let us conclude by pointing out, at least in a general way, some of the implications of all this. We may polarize our remarks around the three foci of this discussion: Piaget, Lacan, Language.

With regard to Piaget, this phenomenological perspective in no way compromises the integrity of his ontic methodology; it simply founds the methodology more deeply than he can do himself. The scientific method supposes an intimacy with the real that its own instruments cannot explore. The knower-known relationship arises subsequent to a more original communion. Furthermore, the Being-dimension of the self that grounds the assimilation-accommodation process of equilibration and structuration is now seen to be an opening up to Being-as-*logos*. Hence, by a natural shift interior to the movement of the philosophical analysis itself, it becomes possible for Piaget's thought to pass from the problem of speech to the problem of language, and (since Being is also the basis of history) to find some way to think, at least on the ontological level, the problems of ontogenesis and phylogenesis together.

As for Lacan, if Being-as-*logos* is really ground for cohesiveness and order, then we do have an ontological "where" for the symbolic order. The musician's insistence on a need for some kind of "unconscious awareness" to be able to understand jazz recalls Lévi-Strauss' metaphorical description of what it is that such unconscious awareness might involve. In comparing the role of the symbolic order in the structuring of myth to that of music with regard to the musicians who both play and listen to it, he writes:

> The music lives out its life in me; I listen to myself through the music. The myth and the musical work thus appear to be like orchestral conductors whose listeners are silent members of the orchestra.[44]

But is an "unconscious awareness" of the symbolic order with its laws all that is meant by Freud's unconscious? This is one of the issues that most needs to be clarified in Lacan. For unconscious processes take place in *man (Dasein)* and Being is not the same as *Dasein,* nor is *Dasein* the same as Being — they are not the "same," at best they are one — with a correlative (not to say "dialectical") oneness. To designate this oneness as "the Other," is not enough to make it clear, it seems to me. Given the present level of understanding, it is difficult to see how the unconscious as *logos* is integrated with the existential-ontological structure of *Dasein* so that we can account for the individually historical dimension of this unconscious — that which is inscribed in the "monument of the body," "the archival documents of childhood memories," "semantic evolution," etc.[45] In any case, what we need is a much more sophisticated anthropology of the self to work with, and a little bit of Piagetian rigor here might help us to develop it.

Moreover, we need a further explanation of the turbulent, chaotic nature of the unconscious that Freud discovered, if we are to be faithful to his thought. Heraclitus already suggests another dimension of Being. Besides *logos,* it is also *polemos* — struggle between opposites, between darkness and light, and (by that very fact) *a-letheia.* Thus, when Being (*logos*) reveals itself in beings, it conceals itself as well, and when man corresponds with it authentically, he must make not only truth but *un*truth his very own.[46] Whether this is sufficient to supply an ontology for "the commonality of irreconcilable opposites," is not for me to say. But I do feel that this conception of *logos-aletheia,* when filtered through the prism of *Dasein*'s own finitude, may account for the lubricity of our experience of truth, for the distortions immanent in the operations of intelligence that are inevitable in the dialectic of equilibration, for the sheer perversity of the unconscious that Lacan sometimes exemplifies better than he elucidates.

Finally, a brief word about speech-language. We began by finding the place where the paths of Piaget and Lacan cross in their joint experience of the first words of a child. Let us end there — and in quite Piagetian fashion. For we know how impressed he was in the beginning of his work by the similarity of a child's conception of physical phenomena to that of the early Greek philosophers, who, in their adulthood, crystallized in their philosophies an experience of the World when our Western intelligence was still young. There is a certain wisdom for us, I suspect, in trying to retrieve the freshness of that experience of our childhood. For both Piaget and Lacan see the initial task of speech to consist not first of all in communicating information but in giving expression to desire by articulating the presence of an absence. To find in Being-as-*logos* the aboriginal Language to which we, through the *logos* in us, respond is to see that *before* language is a system of signs, it is an invocation, a calling into presence, and a celebration of the mystery—alas ineffable—of what it means to *be*.

References

1 Jean Piaget, *Structuralism,* trans. C. Maschler (New York: Harper & Row, 1970), p. 87.

2 *Ibid.,* pp. 3-16.

3. *Ibid.,* pp. 86-87.

4 Jean Piaget and B. Inhelder, *The Psychology of the Child,* trans. H. Weaver (New York: Basic Books, 1969), p. 54.

5 S. Freud "Beyond the Pleasure Principle," in J. Strachey (ed. and trans.) *Standard Edition of the Complete Psychological Works of Sigmund Freud,* Vol. 18 (London: Hogarth Press, 1955; originally published, 1920), pp. 14-15.

6 Jean Piaget and B. Inhelder, *op. cit.,* p. 52.

7 *Ibid.,* p. 52.

8 Jean Piaget, *Structuralism,* p. 81.

9 *Ibid.,* p. 82-83.

10 J. N. Flavell, *The Developmental Psychology of Jean Piaget* (Princeton: Van Nostrand, 1963), p. 36.

11 S. Freud "Beyond the Pleasure Principle," pp. 14-15.

12 J. Lacan, *The Language of the Self: The Function of Language in Psychoanalysis,* trans. A. Wilden (Baltimore: Johns Hopkins, 1968), p. 83.

13 C. Lévi-Strauss, *Structural Anthropology*, trans. C. Jacobson and B. G. Schoepf, (New York: Basic Books, 1963), pp. 58-59.

14 J. Lacan "The Insistence of the Letter in the Unconscious" trans. J. Miel, in R. T. and F. M. de George (eds.) *The Structuralists: From Marx to Lévi-Strauss* (Garden City, N.Y.: Doubleday, 1972), p. 269.

15 R. Jakobson and M. Halle, *Fundamentals of Language* (The Hague: Mouton, 1956), p. 29.

16 J. Lacan, *The Language of the Self: The Function of Language in Psychoanalysis*, p. 83.

17 *Ibid.*, p. 39.

18 R. Jakobson and M. Halle, *Fundamentals of Language*, pp. 53-87.

19 *Ibid.*, pp. 63-75.

20 J. Lacan "The Insistence of the Letter in the Unconscious," pp. 303-310.

21 J. Lacan, *The Language of Self: The Function of Language in Psychoanalysis*, pp. 57-58.

22 *Ibid.*, p. 83.

23 *Ibid.*, p. 40.

24 *Ibid.*, p. 35.

25 *Ibid.*, pp. 35 and 40.

26 *Ibid.*, p. 48.

27 Jean Piaget and B. Inhelder, *The Psychology of the Child*, pp. 111-112.

28 *Ibid.*, p. 114.

29 *Ibid.*, p. 139.

30 *Ibid.*, pp. 139-140.

31 *Ibid.*, p. 69.

32 J. Lacan "The Insistence of the Letter in the Unconscious," p. 312.

33 *Ibid.*, pp. 314, 316.

34 *Ibid.*, p. 314.

35 *Ibid.*, p. 315.

36 M. Heidegger "Logos," trans. J. Lacan, *La Psychoanalyse* 1 (1956): 59-79.

37 Jean Piaget, *Structuralism,* p. 62.

38 *Ibid.*, p. 139.

39 *Ibid.*, p. 140.

40 *Ibid.*, pp. 67-68.

41 M. Heidegger, *Sein und Zeit,* ninth edition (Tübingen: Niemeyer, 1960).

42 M. Heidegger, *Einführung in die Metaphysik* (Tübingen: Niemeyer, 1953), pp. 98-100.

43 M. Heidegger, *Vorträge und Aufsätze* (Pfullingen: Neske, 1954), p. 223.

44 C. Lévi-Strauss. "Overture to *Le Cru et Le Cuit*," trans. J. H. McMahon, in J. Ehrmann (ed.) *Structuralism* (Garden City, N.Y.: Doubleday, 1970), p. 54.

45 J. Lacan, *The Language of the Self: The Function of Language in Psychoanalysis,* p. 21.

46 M. Heidegger, *Sein und Zeit,* p. 299.

Discussion

Hans Furth: I wonder what Lacan thinks about deaf children, who never assimilate the speech of society. If anything, they construct their own gestures. I talked to Chomsky about that, but of course, Chomsky would say that they are born with linguistic competence. So there is no problem for him. But for Lacan, it is a problem to make so much of this speech that comes from society. The existence of a primordial experience that is constitutive of the human being would not be true for deaf children who do not accept speech from society.

William Richardson: I don't know what he would say to that. My own sense of how to respond would be this. He is talking here of a capacity for speech which at least in his existential-logical conception is basically the component of *logos.* The actual exercise of that component depends upon certain auditory images that would be necessary for articulated speech. As I understand him, however, there would be, first of all, a projection of the structures of Being by reason of *Verstehen.* There would be the explicitation of that projection in terms of whatever relatedness the child can have. And there would be, therefore, the possibility of articulating that experience in whatever way is made available to the child or whatever experience it has. It would seem to me, however, that you do have a sense of the liberated quality of the exercise, of the power of words in order to experience presence as. Consider, for example, the "water experience" of Helen Keller, where there is disclosure, experience and a presencing, even though the experience of words and the experience of the world is extremely limited. So I would be forced to say that we are talking about the power to articulate language as indigenous to man rather than the actual exercise of spoken language.

Furth: For deaf children, emulating society's language through individual development is always a big problem. Obviously the deaf child could not develop into a human being unless the deaf child related, communicated and formed symbols. Of course, that is what deaf children do and they do it without language. They create their own means of communication; and they create their own symbols. Precisely because I worked with deaf children, Piaget's theory came to be a framework for making sense of what happens and what I could observe in a majority of cases.

Richardson: I am not sure about taking it beyond Lacan and Heidegger. I am not sure that it is impossible to take language in the sense of the inchoation of speech or the initial moment beyond the barriers of science, that it would not in itself be a kind of communion with things and a type of presencing for the child, a presencing which makes his actual human experience limited and undetected, but which permits the child to manage, at least in a way. He might well give a broader interpretation to the word and to the meaning of articulated language beyond actual formation in the mouth. I cannot cite texts but it seems to me that he has to do that.

Furth: When Piaget speaks of object formation, he includes, of course, the self and other persons. The self exists. Other persons exist. The word "object" does not mean physical object. It means that there is a confrontation between self and other.

Richardson: Yes. The deaf child would certainly have interrelationships with other people as prior to primordial exposure to any thing. The components of the ontological structure would be inhibited. There would be an inchoative speech but not the actual oral expression of it. I am not sure that the oral expression of it is necessary because, although I've never tried to explore this theme in Heidegger myself, there is a tremendous role for silence as a form of language. Basically, silence is a form of letting something be and listening to what it says. In these terms, the deaf child would still interchange with its mother and so forth. According to my hypothesis of really trying to take Lacan at his word and to read the Heideggerian interpretation, it seems that it would be sufficient to be a kind of language, which would therefore be independent of the act of oral emission of words.

Thomas J.J. Altizer: I am enchanted with what you have done with the problem. It seems to be a real *tour de force.* But I would like to share with you this impression. I sense that since your Heidegger book, perhaps through Lacan and structuralism, you have been very much affected by a kind of total thinking. So this thought comes. Deeply-grounded as you are in what, from my point of view, is a totally non-dialectical conception of being, is it possible that Lacan and Lévi-Strauss *et al* have opened to you a totality wherein that very total and truly total non-dialectical conception of Being, when it meets its opposite — namely Lacan's Other — can transpose that opposite into its opposite — *logos* — and therein make it apprehendable by way of Being? In other words, it seems to me that what you do with *logos, Dasein,* and Lacan have nothing to do with Lacan but a great deal to do with William Richardson, Heidegger and the tradition that you represent. To me it is an ingenious, marvelous intellectual achievement and I admire it, but I admire it in terms of its own intellectual dexterity and agility and, let's face it, it makes Lacan mean exactly the opposite of what Lacan presumably means.

Richardson: Well, that's supposing that you know what Lacan presumably means. Maybe it does not, except that the framework which I have worked out, I have worked out *a posteriori.* This is not some antecedent form which I imposed on Lacan. I am impressed by the texts that I have cited here and other texts too. I am not using some sort of cheap trashcan verbiage. I let Heidegger have his word. To let Heidegger have his word is to realize that Lacan translated Heidegger's essay on *logos.* What I was working with tonight was Heidegger's essay on *logos.* I took him at his word. Now if you say to me that this is not a dialectical experience, then I would have to say "Well, maybe." But that limitation is perhaps mine.

Altizer: Is it adequate to Lacan's understanding of the otherness of speech?

Richardson: I think it is for the otherness of speech; but I do not think that it is adequate for the otherness of others—the otherness of people—because at the same time that he develops an ontology of language *à la* Heidegger, he develops a dialectical anthropology so to speak in terms of desire. He has a phrase, which I cannot recall in its full verbal cogency, in which he says that the psychoanalyst has achieved, or even is called to, a great task—combining the man of care with the self of absolute spirit. This means putting together a Heideggerian man who relates dialectically in a Hegelian fashion to other people. That's what he says. But when he comes to developing the dialectic of desire—one of the annoying and perverse things that I find about him is that he is rather cavalier—he is both Heideggerian and Hegelian as well as Freudian . . . and most of all himself! When the chips are down, my greatest suspicion of Lacan is precisely that. This other business about the existential structure of the unconscious can be worked with. Charles Scott has certainly done some work in that area. That is not impossible to do. What I do find very suspicious is the need to put together a Heideggerian ontology with an Hegelian experience of the dialectic. But I am not sure it cannot be done. On the surface, it is not very convincing.

Edward S. Casey: Don't you think that the way Lacan puts it together though is interesting? It seems to me he puts it together by interpreting the grand Other non-dialectically. Actually that is the link between Lacan and Heidegger. The dialectic of desire, though stemming from and expressing a necessarily linguistic framework, is not the same thing as that Other just as beings are not the same thing as Being. One cannot ignore the claim that there is a dialectical relationship between the two, indeed among all the modalities of desire with all the changes which they form and that grand Other which seems to subtend them—at least schematically insofar as he is actually able to conceptualize and verbalize them for us. It reminds me indeed of what one seems to hear from Heidegger, even the early Heidegger—though the problem seems to get much more complex—when you get to the *"logos"* essay where Being which is separate from beings or *logos* is separate from that which comes forth. Heidegger himself then turns to a much more complex and difficult model to which Lacan in his psychoanalytical conception is not faithful. Lacan and Freud are not accidentally paired here with the earlier Heidegger, where there is an absolute diremption between the unconscious or the great Other or Being and whatever else it is that manifests that Being whether we call it desire, language, or interpretations as opposed to understandings. Heidegger poses a more difficult problematic, to which Lacan does not do justice. The reason may simply be that the Freudian system simply does not permit the kind of ontological dialectic which is suggested by Heidegger in the essay on *"logos."*

Richardson: I do not understand what you mean when you say that Lacan is not faithful to the *logos* experience of Heidegger.

Casey: I don't see any way in which Lacan's description of psychoanalytical experience or his reinterpretation of Freud really does introduce the perspectives of that essay on *"logos."* I know that he was influenced by that essay and I know that he takes it seriously. He would say that we should take Heidegger at his word. But I always took that as a kind of capitulation to the later Heidegger, saying: "I cannot incorporate that part of Heidegger into my thinking."

Richardson: It seems to me that his first experience was to be really struck by the *logos* theory, because it did supply an ontological perspective on language. That would permit him to say that language is prior to man. Only subsequently has he played around with Heideggerian terms. That is my sense of it.

Casey: But don't you think that the way that language is prior to man in Lacan is actually much more influenced by Lévi-Strauss and the notion of the symbolic order, which itself seems to fall into a non-dialectical framework — *le nom du père,* something absolutely apart?

Richardson: I am not saying that there is a dialectic in the early Heidegger. I am saying that there is a priority in man which supplies the ground for the symbolic order. And that ground for the symbolic order is there precisely because meaning is language, which is a specifically Heideggerian contribution. It is not really Heraclitus, but Heidegger's reading of the unsaid in Heraclitus.

Charles Scott: Could you say a little more about the relationships that you were suggesting at the end of your paper between mystery, concealment, and Other? I thought you were suggesting that the notions of concealment, emptiness, and Being — that is, non-objective occurrences — were ways in which one might render the inevitability of the Other without absolutizing a dialectic of desire. I don't know whether I heard you correctly or not.

Richardson: That is certainly what I would have wanted to have intended. That says it better than I was saying it myself. I was trying to bring it to terms and it seems to me that the experience that I was trying to articulate is such as you describe, where the mystery—whether it is *logos,* Being, *a-letheia,* or nothing—reveals itself through making it possible. I am trying to do what you have been talking about by bringing into words, in terms of our own interaction, the kind of experience that permits Heidegger to talk the way he does. There is an ontological revelation that takes place precisely through the dialogue. It is a way of listening to the *logos* and seizing the opportunity to bring the whole thing to terms. So I would accept what you say and wish I could have said it that well.

Scott: In this light, you could underscore that, for Lacan, the event of language or language as it happens is simultaneously an occurrence of Other—not in the sense of another person or another thing, but as the occurrence of the absence between the spokes. It is the ungraspable quality that often underlies death analysis. As long as I try in some sense to grasp everything, my life will necessarily be very obsessive and, to the extent that I try to keep everything to me, I will be paranoiac because it escapes. Just those two kinds of examples would indicate the possibility that I understand in Lacan. As articulation occurs, an ungraspableness manifests itself as other than whatever is manifest. That is of major significance when one wants to understand the nature of human consciousness and the human psyche.

Richardson: Yes. I think that that is true. And I think that the analytic process would be an attempt to listen together to that word which is to be uttered. What bothers me about Lacan so far is that the experience of otherness—for all its validity—is something different from the experience of unconscious processes which Freud described. Insofar as there is a meeting point, it seems to me that Lacan has to take account of those processes. That is what I was trying to get at with my notion of *a-letheia,* which, as you know, I find a very powerful idea. Yes, there is a listening to an Other—which is what Heidegger calls: a non-dialectical process that can be viewed in terms of listening to the *logos.* But that is not yet, for my understanding, the dynamic quality of Freud's unconscious, which still has to be taken account of. When things are right, both go together as a unity. We get beyond the conception of analysis as strictly Freudian. On this level, we get closer to the existential approach to treatment such as that we find with Medard Boss. Lacan's structuralism, for all its anti-existentialism, does have some co-naturality with an existential approach to therapy and the possibility of an intersubjective reading. If one can accept the Heideggerian framework, I think Heidegger himself permits us to expand some of Lacan's structures. He certainly permits us to expand some of Freud's structures. And he permits different types of therapy which would be fundamentally much more humane.

Richard Cohen: In the article called the "Principles of Thinking" which Heidegger wrote and which was recently translated in *The Piety of Thinking,* he explains that all serious thinking is dialectical. He does not mean that it has to be the Hegelian dialectic. I mention that not just as a scholarly point, but there are so few words to think about the relationship between the manifest and the dissimulated. I do not think that it is sufficient to just eliminate the word dialectic. It simply eliminates a word that is helpful in thinking about not only the relationship between the ontic and the ontological, but also, at the ontological level, the relationship between the manifest and the dissimulation of the dissimulated. There he does point at a dialectic as a dynamic moving relation.

Richardson: Do you take him to mean that all thought since Hegel is dialectical and his thought is dialectical because it involves an interchange . . .

Cohen: Because it is thinking about itself. That is what Heidegger means here.

Richardson: Does anyone want to sound off on that? He so steadfastly and scrupulously avoided ideally identifying himself with the Hegelian dialectic.

Cohen: He avoids what is specifically the Hegelian dialectic. But in the broad sense, it is thinking turned upon itself and not just a correlation of propositions to objects.

Richardson: If you will excuse me, I would like to see the text. I would also like to know the date of the composition of the text. I will check it out. I cannot identify it from the way you describe it.

Bernard Flynn: If the concept of the unconscious and Heidegger's concept of *a-letheia* have a lot in common it is because they both decenter a subject. In *Being and Time* the relationship between human speech and *logos* could be looked on as a kind of analogy between conscious and unconscious. For example in chapter seven of the *Interpretation of Dreams,* it is not that the unconscious is simply other than or hidden or concealed. It is opposed. It is a focus that operates by a different logic. It is simply Heidegger's concept of *a-letheia.* What is concealed is not fundamentally different from what is revealed. It cannot test presence. It is simply not presence. But for Freud the relationship between the conscious and the unconscious is not that one is conscious and the other is unconscious, but that the unconscious can test consciousness. There is a dynamic relationship between the two. It seems that one can correct a whole negative analogy. In *Being and Time, Dasein* is presented really as a being without an unconscious in the Freudian sense.

Richardson: We would have to explore further what he means by *a-letheia.* My own reading of it has led me to give great weight to *Vom Wesen der Wahrheit* where he talks about the untruth that is first of all *Geheimnis* (Mystery) and secondly *Irre* (the compounding of the mystery). It is as if this darkness or the dark side of Being confounds us, sweeps us up, and therefore founds what Heidegger calls fallenness — our tendency to misinterpret every revelation. The revelation embelishes. Every uncovering is a covering over. Every discovery is a distortion. The perversity of the unconscious is precisely in the notion of *Irre.* That is what I would take to be the basis of the contrariness, the oppositional quality of the unconscious. That is precisely why I find this notion of *a-letheia* very appealing.

Furth: What word are you using for this?

Richardson: Irre. From *irren,* which is sometimes translated as "error." But that is semantics. He is not talking about error. He is talking about the ground of contamination, of chaos, of perversity. My reading of it is very important for politics, for morality and for psychoanalysis.

Furth: Undirected. Lost. Is it not?

Richardson: Yes. It's Being as losing us, as seducing us into our lostness.

Casey: The unconscious for Freud at least is a kind of counter-ground, a counter-logic, which reveals that it has its own intrinsic structure. For the dreamer, for example, there are various mechanisms which Lacan himself has singled out and which are in fact highly orderly. *Irre* seems to suggest a perversity or some form of wandering in lostness and not, finally, a new or counter-ground to consciousness. On the contrary it is more comparable to some kind of strange border being or no-man's land, than to the notion of a separate ground, found elsewhere, and so on. So I wonder how far you would press this analogy.

Richardson: I am not sure that I have pressed it as you are pressing me now. My own sense of it is that the laws of language, as partly discerned by the linguists, do indeed follow a pattern discernible by their ontic measurements — just as intelligence does. There is a quality of confusion in the associations. The polyphony of the associations is sometimes a cacophony. *A-letheia* is its ground.

NOTES ON CONTRIBUTORS

Susan Buck-Morss is Assistant Professor of Government at Cornell University and author of *The Origin of Negative Dialectics: Theodor W. Adorno, Walter Benjamin, and the Frankfurt Institute* (New York: Macmillan, 1977) (Hassocks: Harvester, 1978).

Edward S. Casey is Professor of Philosophy at the State University of New York at Stony Brook, author of *Imagining: A Phenomenological Study* (Bloomington: Indiana University Press, 1976), and translator of two major books by Mikel Dufrenne.

Hans G. Furth is Professor of Psychology at the Catholic University of America and author of *Thinking Without Language: Psychological Implications of Deafness* (New York: Free Press, 1966), *Piaget and Knowledge* (Englewood Cliffs, New Jersey: Prentice-Hall, 1969), *Piaget for Teachers* (Englewood Cliffs, New Jersey: Prentice-Hall, 1970) and *Deafness and Learning* (Belmont, California: Wadsworth, 1973).

William J. Richardson, S.J. is Professor of Philosophy at Fordham University and Director of Research at the Austen Riggs Center. He is author of *Heidegger: Through Phenomenology to Thought* (The Hague: Nijhoff, 1963) and several articles on the philosophical foundations of psychotherapy.

Charles E. Scott is Professor of Philosophy at Vanderbilt University, author of essays in existential phenomenology, and co-editor of *Heidegger: In Europe and America* (The Hague: Nijhoff, 1973) and the Fall 1977 issue of *Soundings* on *Approaches to Dreaming: An Encounter with Medard Boss*.

Index of Participants

Index of Authors

Abraham, Iggeret Magen, 135
Achebe, Chinva, 133
Adorno, Theodor, x, xi, 103-143, 171
Ariès, Philippe, 121, 136
Aristotle, 38, 68-69, 71, 75, 93, 97-98
Arnold, W.J., 129

Beethoven, Ludwig, 111, 142
Benjamin, Walter, 103, 113, 125-127, 141-142, 170
Berg, Alban, 108
Bergson, Henri, 74, 84-86, 95, 140
Berry, Boyd M., 136
Bloom, Harold, 127
Bloomfield, Leonard, 146
Boethius, vii
Boss, Medard, viii, 18, 168
Bourbaki, 49
Brée, Germaine, 127
Breuer, Joseph, 68
Brown, Norman O., 21, 134-135
Buck-Morss, Susan, x, 125-127, 132
Butor, Michel, 135-136

Casey, Edward S., ix, 31
Chomsky, Noam, 112, 131, 146, 157, 163
Chukovsky, Kornei, 113, 131-132
Collaer, Paul, 127

Datan, H., 127
Dante Aligheri, vii
Darwin, Charles, 49
Dasen, P.R., 125
DeGeorge, R. & F., 162

Descartes, René, 32, 58, 69
Dewey, John, 53
Douglas, Mary, 134
Duckworth, Eleanor, 128
Dufrenne, Mikel, 171
Durkheim, Emile, 109, 128, 153

Ehrmann, Jacques, 163
Einstein, Albert, 58, 140
Engels, Friedrich, 107, 129, 140
Erickson, Erik, 17
Escher, M. C., 111
Euclid, 50, 58, 111
Evans-Pritchard, E. E., 109

Flavell, John N., 161
Foucault, Michel, viii-ix, xi, 16, 18-29, 32-34, 139
Freud, Sigmund, ix, xi, 18, 43, 63-102, 122, 129, 140, 145, 147-148, 151-152, 155, 160-161, 166, 168-169
Fromm, Erich, 136
Furth, Hans, vii-viii, 10, 39

Gadamer, Hans-Georg, 22, 27, 32, 61
Gödel, Kurt, 50
Goslin, D. A., 126
Gouldner, Alvin W., 128
Gras, Vernon, 135

Habermas, Jürgen, 117, 119-120, 133, 135
Halle, Morris, 149, 162
Harris, Joel Chandler, 133-134
Hegel, G.W.F., 21, 25, 32, 107, 117, 120, 126, 129, 135, 166, 169